Publications on Asia
of the
Institute for Comparative
and Foreign Area Studies

NUMBER 28

Hellmut Wilhelm, professor emeritus of Chinese literature and history at the University of Washington, has written many articles and books, including *Change: Eight Lectures on the I Ching* and *The Book of Changes in the Western Tradition: A Selective Bibliography*.

WILHELM, Hellmut. Heaven, earth, and man in the Book of changes: seven Eranos lectures. University of Washington, 1977. 230p (Publications on Asia of the Institute for Comparative and Foreign Area Studies, no. 28) index 76-7801. 12.95 ISBN 0-295-95516-3. C.I.P.

CHOICE   NOV. '77
Philosophy

Wilhelm, professor emeritus at the University of Washington and a noted authority on the *Book of changes* ("I Ching"), brings together seven papers he originally delivered at the Eranos conferences in Switzerland between 1951 and 1967. The appearance of these lectures together in English for the first time is welcome. While Wilhelm's *Change: eight lectures on the I Ching* (1960) is an excellent introduction to the *Book of changes* as a whole, the Eranos lectures each explore significant concepts and images from the text. Topics covered include the creative principle, wanderings of the spirit, and the building of one's own city as a stage of formation. The essays on the concept of time, human events and their meaning, and the interaction of heaven, earth, and man in the *I Ching* and Yang Hsiung are especially insightful. Though likely of concern only to those with specialized interest in the *I Ching*, the essays are clear, well written, and sufficiently nontechnical to be of use to undergraduates. Recommended for libraries wishing collections strong on classical China.

306

This book is sponsored by the China Colloquium of the Institute for Comparative and Foreign Area Studies.

HELLMUT WILHELM

Heaven, Earth, and Man
in the Book of Changes

SEVEN ERANOS LECTURES

UNIVERSITY OF WASHINGTON PRESS
SEATTLE AND LONDON

Library of Congress Cataloging in Publication Data

Wilhelm, Hellmut, 1905–
   Heaven, earth, and man in The book of changes.

   (Publications on Asia of the Institute for
Comparative and Foreign Area Studies; no. 28)
   Includes index.
    1. I ching. I. I ching. II. Title.
III. Series: Washington (State). University.
Institute for Comparative and Foreign Area Studies.
Publications on Asia; no. 28.
PL2464.Z7W55   299′.5128′2   76–7801
ISBN 0–295–95516–3

PREFACE

There is contained in the Great Treatise of the Book of Changes
a passage in verse that goes like this:

> The Changes is a book
> From which one cannot hold aloof.
> Its Tao
> Is forever changing,
> Alteration, movement without rest,
> Flowing through the six empty places;
> Rising and sinking without fixed law,
> Firm and yielding transform each other.
> They cannot be confined within a rule;
> It is only change that is at work here.[1]

The first statement of this passage is meant as an admonition;
it is, however, at the same time a statement of fact. Whoever has
realized what the Book has to offer, be he a philosopher, a social
reformer, or a pragmatic statesman, even an empire builder, will

1. See *The I Ching* or Book of Changes. The Richard Wilhelm Translation
rendered into English by Cary F. Baynes, 3rd ed. (Princeton: Princeton University Press, 1967, and later printings), p. 348 (hereafter cited as Wilhelm-
Baynes).

[v]

not be able to let go again. This specific attractiveness of the Book is evident in all periods; it has captivated an ever widening circle of heedful students, a circle, for that matter, that has recently grown considerably. That the Book of Changes was then considered the first among the Chinese Classics has, without doubt, added to its authority. It appears, however, that it was not so much this "authority," but rather its content that kept people from holding aloof, even that the "authority" was at times in the way of a genuine and immediate understanding.

In my own case, this fascination is an inherited as much as an acquired trait. It thus filled me with supreme satisfaction when I was invited, in 1951 to participate in the Eranos Meetings in order to present what the Book had to contribute to the general themes of these meetings.

The Eranos Meetings owe their establishment to the vision of a very remarkable woman: Olga Froebe-Kapteyn (1881–1962). In the planning stage, she had requested and received the assistance of the well-known comparative religionist Rudolf Otto (1869–1937). It was he who contributed the name "Eranos," linking the new idea to the classical academies, their discussions, and their feasts.[2]

Eranos, then, provided a meeting place for the representatives of all cultures and of all disciplines, including the humanities as well as the exact sciences, where contributions of a most varied nature on a given general topic were presented to an interested audience. Beginning with the first meeting in 1933, C. G. Jung was a frequent contributor and many of his seminal ideas were first developed at these Eranos Meetings. Over 120 different speakers

2. There are a number of essays on the Eranos Meetings, such as: Walter Robert Corti, *Zwanzig Jahre Eranos* (Zurich: Rhein-Verlag, 1951); Olga Froebe-Kapteyn, *25 Jahre Eranos* (Zurich: Rhein-Verlag, 1957); Adolf Portmann, *Vom Sinn und Auftrag der Eranos-Tagungen* (Zurich: Rhein-Verlag, 1961); *Mircea Eliade and Ira Progoff about the Eranos Conferences* (Ascona: Casa Eranos, 1967).

have appeared here over the years. After the death of Olga Froebe, the meetings were arranged by Adolf Portmann (a biologist) with the assistance of Rudolf Ritsema (an *I ching* expert).

I personally appeared at Eranos seven times, lecturing as a rule in German; only my last lecture, in 1967, was given in English.[3] In this volume, English versions of these seven lectures are submitted. They might, in their own way, show some of the relevant images and concepts of the Book of Changes, and it is hoped that they do it in the spirit of Eranos.

"The Concept of Time" was read to the Eranos Meeting of 1951. The general theme of this meeting was "Mensch und Zeit" (Man and Time). The essay was first published in *Eranos Jahrbuch 1951*, 20: 231–48 (Zurich: Rhein-Verlag, 1952). The English translation is by Ralph Manheim. It was revised by Cary F. Baynes and was first published in Joseph Campbell, ed., *Papers from the Eranos Yearbooks*, vol. 3, *Man and Time*, Bollingen Series, no. 30, pp. 212–32 (New York: Pantheon Books, 1957). This is, with slight changes, the version presented. It is reprinted here with the permission of Princeton University Press.

"The Creative Principle" was presented at the Eranos Meeting of 1956, whose general theme was "Der Mensch und das Schöpferische" (Man and the Creative Principle). It was first published in *Eranos Jahrbuch 1956*, 25: 455–75 (Zurich: Rhein-Verlag, 1957). The English translation is by Jane A. Pratt and Marianne Cowan and was first published in *Spring 1970*, pp. 91–110. It is reprinted here, with slight changes, with the permission of Spring Publications.

"Human Events and Their Meaning" was presented under the title "Der Sinn des Geschehens nach dem Buch der Wandlungen" at the Eranos Meeting of 1957, whose general theme was "Mensch und Sinn" (Man and Meaning). It was first published in *Eranos*

3. A German version of these lectures appeared under the title *Sinn des I Ging* (Düsseldorf-Cologne: Diederichs, 1972).

Jahrbuch 1957, 26: 351–86 (Zurich: Rhein-Verlag, 1958). The English translation is by Hildegard Kaufmann and Max von Hollweg.

"The Own City as the Stage of Formation" was presented at the Eranos Meeting of 1960, whose general theme was "Mensch und Gestaltung" (Man and Creative Form). It was first published in *Eranos Jahrbuch 1960*, 29: 207–42 (Zurich: Rhein-Verlag, 1961). The English translation is by Hildegard Kaufmann and Crispin Wilhelm.

"The Interaction of Heaven, Earth, and Man" was presented at the Eranos Meeting of 1962, which had the theme of "Der Mensch, Führer and Geführter im Werk" (Man, Leader and Led). It was first published in *Eranos Jahrbuch 1962*, 31: 317–50 (Zurich: Rhein-Verlag, 1963). The English translation is by Richard H. Gottlieb and Crispin Wilhelm.

"Wanderings of the Spirit" was presented to the Eranos Meeting of 1964, whose general theme was "Das menschliche Drama in der Welt der Ideen" (The Human Drama in the World of Ideas). It was first published in *Eranos Jahrbuch 1964*, 33: 178–200 (Zurich: Rhein-Verlag, 1965). The English translation is by Hildegard Kaufmann and Crispin Wilhelm. It was first published in *Spring 1974*, pp. 80–101, and is reprinted here with the permission of Spring Publications.

"The Interplay of Image and Concept" was presented (in English) at the Eranos Meeting of 1967, whose general theme was "Polarität des Lebens" (Polarity of Life). It was first published in *Eranos Jahrbuch 1967*, 36: 31–57 (Zurich: Rhein-Verlag, 1968).

In addition to thanking the publishers who have given me permission to reprint these selections, I wish also to thank Wing-tsit Chan, David Hawkes, Gerald W. Swanson, Derk Bodde, and George W. Kent for permission to use selections from translations they have made, Princeton University Press for allowing me to quote from Fung Yu-lan, *The Period of Classical Learning*, vol. 2 of *A History of Chinese Philosophy*, translated by Derk Bodde, and George Allen & Unwin, Ltd., and Barnes & Noble, publishers of the works of the late Arthur Waley, for permission to quote a translation of a poem and from his book *The Way and Its Power*.

CONTENTS

Heaven, Earth, and Man
in the Book of Changes

I

THE CONCEPT OF TIME

I

The system of existence and events underlying the Book of Changes lays claim to completeness. The book attempts a correlation of the situations of life in all strata, personal and collective, and in all dimensions. An added feature of the system are the trends of development latent within the various situations and their reciprocal relations. The implications of this second aspect of the book—which reveal, among other things, that none of the sixty-four situations given can be conceived altogether statically—have been so stressed that we have grown accustomed to understand the word *J* of the title as meaning "change." Though this translation certainly comes very close to the meaning of the word both in a logical and an empirical sense, we must not forget that the concept *J* as such connotes not only the dynamic aspect of life, but also what is firm, reliable, and irrevocable in the system of coordinates it covers. An early apocryphon states as much in the paradoxical definition: "Change: that is the unchangeable."[1]

1. See Hellmut Wilhelm, *Change: Eight Lectures on the J Ching*, Bollingen Series, no. 62 (Princeton, N.J.: Princeton University Press, 1960), pp. 20–21. It is not even certain that we are justified in retaining the derivation of the

We need to focus on this logical aspect of the system if we wish to discover the laws that govern it. The book lends itself readily to such speculation. This was the aspect that again and again occupied the minds of the commentators when China's stage of social development inclined toward rigidity, as in the days of the Han, and especially during the Sung dynasty, when justification for the systematization of social dependencies was sought in the Book of Changes. The early masters of Sung philosophy, who all based their systems on this book, uniformly stressed the elements that persist even in change. Chou Tun-i, the founder of this new philosophical trend, saw the development inherent within the concept J in terms of hierarchical images whose temporal sequence is paralleled by a systematic scale of values; from the supreme pole the two basic powers of yang and yin emanate, from their interaction the five states of change result, and the relations between these five in turn give rise to the world of existence.[2] Here, then, change is seen in a temporal schema that not only is unilinear but also incorporates a rigid hierarchical scale. Such an image is not unimpressive; it could be applied to systems of dependencies outside philosophy and be brought to bear on social relations as well as on intellectual life. This fact contributed to the dominant position of Sung philosophy in subsequent Chinese history.

Thus it is evident that the emphasis on the uniform and the regular in the process of change in time represents a danger. The projection of change into the "unchangeable" finds expression here in spatial images of the relation between above and below. Thus the conception rests on a mixture of two categories, time and

character J from the picture of the lizard as a mobile, changing animal; studies of recently discovered material suggest that the word is derived from the concept of the fixed and straight, hence also of the directional. I am indebted to my colleague Erwin Reifler for this reference.

2. Georg von der Gabelentz, *Thai-kih-thu des Tscheu Tse, Tafel des Urprinzips mit Tschu Hi's Commentare* (Dresden, 1876).

space. An attempt is made to understand the temporal in spatial terms. Thinking influenced by hierarchical feeling superimposes one dimension of space on that of time. The origin of this fallacy is easy to grasp: the logic of an order easily established in space leads to the wish for an analogous mastery of time that is much more difficult to order—and it was thought that this could be accomplished through borrowing from spatial modes of thought.

Clearly, the concept of change itself does not lend itself to systematic interpretation, but the world conception set forth in the sixty-four images of the *I ching* remains open to such an approach and, indeed, calls for it. The idea on which this book is based— that questions at the dark gate are to be answered not by the intuition of an oracular priest or priestess, however well equipped, but by a collection of written texts—is valid only if these texts form a self-contained, exhaustive whole; in other words, only if every questioner may find a correspondent answer for every question. This idea is still relatively easy to apprehend if one expects nothing more from the answers than a guide within a definite culture at a definite epoch. After all, it was the creators of this culture, or at least groups close to them, who formulated these texts. But the *I ching* is not merely a handbook of possible situations and a guide to possible behavior for the early Chou period; it has been used successfully both in other periods and in other cultures. This opens up an aspect of the book that can no longer be explained by saying that the creator of a culture is in a position to ordain the proper form of behavior within the culture. It is striking, for example, that although the *I ching* contains memories of exemplary situations from the early history of the Chou dynasty, we find no passages that draw rigid inferences from the typical feudalistic structure of early Chou society. On the contrary, the situations are always raised above temporal manifestations into a realm where they bear an archetypal character; historical recollections

[5]

are used to illustrate the archetype but never to tie it to a particular manifestation. Thus the system of the texts appears timeless, or above time.

Of course, this does not answer the question of how it was possible to create a system of archetypes that can lay claim to completeness. Probably we shall not be able to provide an answer here. It would be necessary to take up in detail the early history of the Chou, who at the time the early strata of the book took form were still close to the dazzling starlight of the high steppes, though their economy had recently shifted to an emphasis on agriculture, under circumstances in which a trusting reliance on nature had to be complemented by artificial, communally directed irrigation projects. Such experiences produced a mind open to the primary questions of human existence.[3] This openness of mind meant a freedom from prejudice toward answers that came from other spheres, for example, from the culturally far superior Shang Empire, which the Chou were soon to subjugate, or —perhaps still more important—from their southwestern neighbors in present-day Tibet.[4]

Another of the old masters of Sung philosophy, Shao Yung, who is usually regarded as the father of the idealistic school in this philosophy, made the system of archetypes of the J ching, embodied in the sixty-four hexagrams, a subject of his speculation. He was attracted by the step-by-step progression of the situation within the hexagram, expressed by successive whole or divided lines, and he attempted, by a systematization of this progression within the individual hexagram, to create a new "natural" system of all sixty-four. The essential element of his analysis was the

3. On this point see *Spring 1972* (Zurich), pp. 75–76.

4. Wolfram Eberhard was the first to call attention to these influences in the Book of Changes. See his *Lokalkulturen im alten China* (Leiden, 1942), 1:290–94. His argument there perhaps requires to be worked out in greater detail. Nonetheless his thesis remains extremely suggestive.

whole and broken—yang and yin—lines, from which, viewing them at first in a strictly graphic sense, he constructed the individual hexagram and with it his new system of the hexagrams.

Starting with the two primary lines, yang and yin, he obtains the fundamental line of the individual hexagram and a twofold division of the whole system:

Then he adds above each of the two a yang line and a yin line. With this the individual sign gains in complexity, and the total system is divided into four:

At first merely graphic images, these four line complexes also suggest an analysis from the standpoint of content; they are called the big yang, the little yang, the little yin, and the big yin—the lowest line in each case determines their character. To each line complex is now added a yang line and, again, a yin line: an eight-fold division is obtained, consisting of trigrams in the following new arrangement:

Through the addition once again of a yang line and a yin line, the following picture results:

$+ 8$
$= 16$

The addition for the fifth time of a yang and a yin line yields the following:

$+ 24$
$= 32$

And when the simultaneous progression arrives at the last line, the sixty-four hexagrams stand in this new order:

$+ 56$
$= 64$

the last eight being:

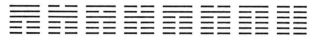

Shao Yung arranged this new system in various ways. To the linear order beginning with Ch'ien and ending with K'un he added a square order in which eight rows, each of eight hexagrams, are placed one above the other so that the ninth, seventeenth, twenty-fifth, and so on stand over the first hexagram; the tenth, eighteenth, twenty-sixth, and so on over the second hexagram, and so on. It then develops that the horizontal rows always have the lower trigram in common, while the vertical rows have the upper one in common. Finally, he arranged them in a circular form; here, if the second half of his series is stood on its head, a correspondence results with the so-called Earlier Heaven order of the eight trigrams.[5]

This restructuring and resystematization of the hexagrams appear to have grown out of a speculation on graphic images. However, it is worth noting that this artificial construction facilitates insights into the locus of a situation characterized by the hexagram (that is to say, into the place of the situation within the system), into the significance of the individual line, and into affinities between the various hexagrams.

It was this aspect of the system that Leibniz happened upon. In the course of his correspondence with Father Bouvet, one of the group of Jesuits who were then active at the court in Peking, Bouvet sent him a chart bearing the square as well as the circular arrangement of Shao Yung. The contemplation of this table led Leibniz to establish a correspondence disclosing one of the most amazing parallelisms between Eastern and Western thought. Some years earlier Leibniz had made use of a new numerical system that was meant to facilitate the computation of tangential magnitudes. This so-called binary system corresponds in principle to the usual

5. Wilhelm-Baynes, p. 266.

[8]

decimal system but makes use of only two figures, 1 and 0. The numerical sequence of the binary system would look as follows: 1, 10, 11, 100, 101, 111, 1000, and so forth.

For Leibniz this system had a significance beyond that of a mathematical aid. He did not regard the events of life and the categories of thought as exhausted by time, space, and causality but apprehended all existence also from the standpoint of pre-established harmony. To his wide-ranging mind, number and the numerical system therefore had more than an abstract meaning; they were expressive of connotative associations that have long since fallen into oblivion. Of course we, too, make use of numbers and numerical formulas to express laws in the physical world —the orbit of the moon, for example, or the organization of a flower. But Leibniz attempted more; with the help of numbers he attempted to trace the laws of spiritual truths as well. Spiritual realities, he argued, can become convincing beyond question only if represented in numbers. His pre-established harmony provided the foundation that enabled him without hesitation to associate number with concepts that extend beyond the physical world. In his binary system the number 1 stood for the creative unity (*unité*), whose highest expression is God, and 0 for the nothingness of unformed chaos.

In Leibniz's mind the equation of Shao Yung's arrangement of the sixty-four hexagrams with his own system was immediately consummated. He took the broken line for a 0 and the unbroken line for a 1 and, by disregarding any zeros preceding 1, arrived at a perfect correspondence between the two series. But this correspondence presents two anomalies. First, Leibniz was compelled to draw in the 0 and set it at the beginning of his system, even before the 1. The order would then be: 0, 1, 10, 11, 100, 101, and so forth. This means that the "nothingness of unformed chaos," which in Leibniz's system occurs not by itself but only in relation to the "creative unity," had to be absolutized and placed before the unity. Thus posited, it gains decisive importance. The second anomaly is that the correspondence is inverse rather than direct. Shao Yung's last sign occupies the first place in Leibniz's system, and his first sign occupies last place. Leibniz himself does not seem to have been aware of this; Father Bouvet's chart did not enable him to distinguish which was the beginning and which the end in the Chinese system. But to us the inversion of the correspondence seems characteristic of the relation between Western and Eastern thinking.[6]

Leibniz's discovery could be said to imply that the hexagrams, as differentiations of a harmonious and systematic whole, are not posited at random but occupy consequent loci. This would mean that they are not chance lots drawn from a grab bag but dispositions in a meaningful complex.

Leibniz himself was well aware of the significance of such conclusions. He assumed that the meaningful character of the position of the hexagram must be manifested in its name and content. (The textual meaning of the hexagrams is indeed entirely in accord with their line structure.) It is doubtful whether he ever obtained corroboration of these assumptions, and his discovery therefore remained in the nature of an episode, but it throws a clear light on the system of the Book of Changes, which in this aspect is a system developing in time, progressing step by step. It might be added that this temporally unilinear progression is predicated on the speculation of Shao Yung, who transposed the book's a posteriori order (the "Order of Later Heaven") into an a priori order (the "Order of Earlier Heaven"). In the (a posteriori, em-

6. Leibniz published his discovery of this correspondence in a memorial of the *Paris Academy* (1703), 3:85 ff. I discussed the correspondence between Leibniz and Father Bouvet in "Leibniz and the I-ching," *Collectanea Commissionis Synodalis* (Peking), 16 (1943) : 205—19. For further literature on this intriguing question see *The Book of Changes in the Western Tradition: A Selective Bibliography*. *Parerga*, no. 2 (Seattle: University of Washington, Institute for Comparative and Foreign Area Studies, 1975).

pirical) Order of Later Heaven the relation in time of hexagram to hexagram is more obscure than in the (a priori, logical) Order of Earlier Heaven. And this characterizes the difference between immediately experienced time (of sense perception) and abstract time (of mathematics). The latter is also included in the Book of Changes, though in veiled form; the oracle seeker, however, prefers to leave this aspect of time to logical speculation and to concentrate on the experienced situation manifested in the sign he has drawn.

Indeed, the problem of how an oracle actually comes into being, of how a question becomes coordinated with the correct answer from the text of the book, can be solved only if a system is presupposed. Without a system, the synchronicity[7] of answer and question would seem if not wholly the play of chance, at least dimly defined. The oracle seeker may be content with a vague harmony if only the answer applies to his question; but the institution of the oracle requires a firmer foundation. Where this order is sought is less important than the fact of its existence. One may find it in the Leibnizian category of pre-established harmony, in which the harmonious and parallel order of events is assumed to be fixed, or one may accept his idea that laws expressible in numbers underlie all truths and not merely those of the physical world.

Wang Fu-chih (1619–92 A.D.) has given us a theory of the oracle more in keeping with the second possibility. His premise is an ordered continuum of existence, which is governed by laws and is all-embracing. This continuum "lacks appearance"—that is, it is not immediately accessible to sense perception. But through the dynamism inherent in existence, images are differentiated out of the continuum that by their structure and position partake of the laws of the continuum; they are, in a sense, individuations of this continuum. On the one hand, these images— that is, the sixty-

7. Cf. C. G. Jung, "Über Synchronizität," *Eranos Jahrbuch 1951*, 20 (1952): 271–84, and also later programmatic statements of Jungian Synchronicity.

four situations of the Book of Changes—can be perceived and experienced; on the other hand, as embodiments of the law and therefore governed by it, they are open to theoretical speculation. With this they enter into the field of numbers and may be numerically structured and ordered as objects of theory governed by law. Thus each situation can be apprehended in two ways: through direct experience as a consequence of the dynamism of existence, and through theoretical speculation as a consequence of the continuousness of existence and its government by laws. The oracle serves to bring the two aspects into harmony with each other, to coordinate a question resulting from immediate, differentiated experience, with the theoretically correct—and the only correct—answer. The questioner thus obtains access to the theoretically established aspect of his own situation, and by reference to the texts set forth under this aspect in the Book of Changes he obtains counsel and guidance from the experience of former generations and the insights of the great masters. Thus the synchronicity disclosed by the oracle is merely the apprehension of two different modes of experiencing the same state of affairs.[8]

This explanation—here somewhat expanded—by Wang Fu-chih has been generally accepted in China, but various things in it may disturb us. First of all, it may trouble us that this explanation was not thought out until some two thousand years after the completion of the Book of Changes. Yet in this connection we might recall a word of Confucius when someone asked him for an explanation of the Grand Sacrifice: " 'I cannot give one. Any person who would know how to explain it would have the world right here.' And he pointed to the palm of his hand."[9] The evidently very complicated Grand Sacrifice existed, and in the opinion of Confucius had a

8. On this point see *Change*, pp. 97–98.
9. Analects 3.2; James R. Ware, trans., *The Best of Confucius* (Garden City, N.Y.: Doubleday & Co., 1950), p. 33.

meaning that, if known, would have elucidated the world order. And yet this meaning was not known. For if anyone had known it, it would have been Confucius, who was more concerned with the form and significance of rites than anyone else in his day. Similar examples might be adduced from other cultures. It would seem that social institutions rise and grow and fulfill their function, although the meaning of this function is not necessarily known and the institutions not necessarily devised on the basis of this meaning. Hence it need not trouble us if such a meaning is not distilled from the form and function of the institution until a much later period.

But this does not help us over another difficulty: how is it possible that numbers and numerical formulas arrived at by a throwing of coins or a manipulation of yarrow stalks should disclose a relation that establishes a man's own fate in time and accounts for its development? That a toss of the coins or a division of a bundle of yarrow stalks should achieve such a result seems to us to relegate the oracle to the realm of coincidence. For us in the West it is hard to see how a genuine synchronicity could be arrived at by so seemingly mechanical a means.

Obviously Wang Fu-chih was also aware of the rational difficulty back of this doubt. For him number and numerical formulas were tools, and the manner in which they were obtained was method. Of course this method, if incorrectly applied, is just as likely to obscure the law as to reveal it. Something more is needed to put one in a position to make proper use of the tools and the method. It is not something that can be rationally induced at will; it is an attitude, through which the tools and the method can be brought to bear effectively. Indeed, modern psychology also has noted the existence of a particular attitude through which synchronicity can be apprehended; there must be an openness to such connections. Unlike the psychologists, however, Wang Fu-chih designated the requisite attitude "integrity." "Only a man of the highest integrity," he says, "can understand this law; basing himself on its revelation he can grasp the symbols, and observing its small expressions he can understand the auguries."

Thus the law is revealed only to the man of integrity; he alone can grasp the connection existing between experience and the meaning of what has been experienced; only he can apply the method to read the tendencies of events from small manifestations. For this no special wisdom is needed and no special experience; it is not the prerogative of a privileged or specially trained group; no priest is made into the administrator or interpreter of human destiny; no mystical immersion is the bridge to a mysterious vision. All that is needed is integrity, a willingness to see things as they are, the attitude of one who does not fool himself or others and does not hide behind conventional or sophisticated rationalizations. Given this intense awareness and openness to the reality of events, the tools and the method become a means of bringing experience into harmony with meaning, present with future.

Of course, this does not mean it is advisable to disregard tools and method. As we have said, a number is that manifestation of any law by which it can be apprehended. The sixty-four hexagrams are built up of lines that have numerical values, and the method of drawing the hexagrams by lot is based on the use of numbers. The method itself incorporates certain fundamental insights into the nature of existence and development, and these insights in turn are expressed by numbers and by the frequency of a possible numerical combination. Both of the methods employed, the throwing of coins and the manipulation of yarrow stalks, contain these insights; the former embodies them in a somewhat crude, the latter in a far more differentiated, form. A compilation of the possible results of the toss of the three coins (as we know, the side with the inscription on it is counted as two and the other side as three) makes this clear. The eight possibilities that can emerge from a toss of the coins are distributed among the line numbers as follows:

one possible occurrence of a six (changing yin line)

three possible occurrences of a seven (resting yang line)

three possible occurrences of an eight (resting yin line)

one possible occurrence of a nine (changing yang line)

These possibilities embody certain trends of probability. The probability of throwing a resting line rather than a changing line is three to one. The probability of throwing a yin line rather than a yang line is one to one.

But a more greatly differentiated law of probability is operative in the yarrow stalk method. Here the possible results for a line are not eight but sixty-four, which are distributed among the line numbers as follows:

four possible occurrences of a six

twenty possible occurrences of a seven

twenty-eight possible occurrences of an eight

twelve possible occurrences of a nine

Here, too, the probability of a yang line (20+12) and of a yin line (28+4) is one to one, and the relation of the resting line (20+28) to the changing (4+12) line is three to one. But a further probability is incorporated in this method, namely, that rest and change are diversely distributed between yin and yang, so that the yang is more inclined (3:5) toward change than is the yin (1:7).[10]

II

As an introduction to the way in which the aspect of time is expressed in the texts of the Book of Changes, and to the part

10. Mathematical probabilities involved in the method of consulting the oracle have recently been discussed a great deal. For an advanced computation of these probabilities see Leo Reisinger, *Das J Ging: eine formalwissenschafteiche Untersuchung des chinesischen Orakels* (Vienna: Stiglmayer, 1972).

played by time in the situations described, we select two quotations that throw light on the special nature of the time element. The first is taken from Hexagram 4, *Meng*, Youthful Folly:

	above	Ken	Keeping Still, Mountain
	below	K'an	The Abysmal, Water

Here, much to the dismay of the aged and the wise, the Judgment says: "Youthful folly has success."[11] The Commentary on the Decision explains this statement with the words: "That he succeeds in his action is due to his hitting time [in the bull's-eye]."[12]

Thus the success of the young fool's actions is attributed here to his being more in harmony with time than the old and wise, whose experience and dogmas may hinder them in this respect. The spontaneous, unreflecting attitude of the young fool enables him to maintain himself in the heart (center) of time. And the time element of this situation is so strong a factor in its unfolding that even the folly of youth cannot obstruct it. (The texts of this hexagram make it perfectly clear that we are concerned here not with a youthful genius but truly with a fool.)

The second quotation is taken from Hexagram 63, *Chi Chi*, After Completion:

	above	K'an	The Abysmal, Water
	below	Li	The Clinging, Fire

Here, under nine in the fifth place, a situation is described that occurs also in the religions of other cultures: the neighbor in the east, who slaughters an ox, does not attain as much real happiness as the neighbor in the west with his small offering. The Commentary on the Images to this text says: "The eastern neighbor, who slaughters an ox, is not as much in harmony with the time as the

11. Wilhelm-Baynes, p. 20.
12. Cf. ibid., p. 406.

western neighbor."[13] This explanation is surprising. The difference in the outcome of the sacrifice depends not on the attitude of the sacrificer, as one might expect, but on the timing (*Zeitgemässheit*) of the sacrifice. This throws light not only on the institution of sacrifice in itself and on the attitude of the sacrificer, but again on the time factor in a given situation.

The conception of time that we encounter in these quotations is very concrete. Here time is immediately experienced and perceived. It does not represent merely a principle of abstract progression but is fulfilled in each of its segments; an effective agent not only in which reality is enacted but which in turn acts on reality and brings it to completion. Just as space appears to the concrete mind not merely as a schema of extension but as something filled with hills, lakes, and plains—in each of its parts open to different possibilities—so time is here taken as something filled, pregnant with possibilities, which vary with its different moments and which, magically as it were, induce and confirm events. Time here is provided with attributes to which events stand in a relation of right or wrong, favorable or unfavorable.

A more abstract concept of time was not unknown in China of that period. At the time of the later strata of the Book of Changes, to which the commentaries we have just quoted belong, we find evidence of a mathematical-astronomical concept of time that served as a foundation for a highly developed science of the calendar; we also have the record of a space-time schema, in which time was regarded as one of the coordinates of extension.[14] But the Book of Changes eschews such theoretical concepts of time, oper-

13. Ibid., p. 713.

14. See Eduard Erkes, "Antithetische Komposition und Dekomposition im Chinesischen," *Sinologica* (Basel), 2 (1950) :132n. A similar passage is found in *Shih-tzu*, who lived in the 4th century B.C.; see Sun Hsing-yen's ed., *chüan* 2, fragment 50.

ating with the word *shih*, "time," in a manner that is much closer to its derivation. The word meant originally "sowing time," then "season" in general (cf. French, *saison*, Latin, *satio*). In its early form it was composed of the character for "sole of the foot" (Latin, *planta*) above that for a unit of measurement.[15] In China, too, the sole of the foot is related semantically to planting; thus, the word means a section of time set apart for a certain activity. Thence its meaning was extended to the four seasons, all of which are correspondingly filled with certain activities, and only then to time in general. The word is often used in the Book of Changes in the meaning of "season," and many of the characteristic attributes of time can be traced to this heritage.

Thus it is often said that the seasons do not err[16] and that therefore the great man takes them as a model for his consistent behavior.[17] They derive two of their most important characteristics from the ordered revolution of heaven and earth.[18] From it they derive their unremitting change as well as their consistent continuity. In the Great Treatise this is expressed as follows: "There is nothing that has more movement or greater cohesion than the four seasons." And "The changes and continuity correspond to [literally, "are correlated with"] the four seasons."[19] Change is not only something that happens to them or in them, but also something that influences the happening: "The four seasons change and transform, and thus can forever bring to completion."[20]

15. I am again indebted to Erwin Reifler for this information.

16. Commentary on the Decision: Hex. 16, Enthusiasm, and Hex. 20, Contemplation (Wilhelm-Baynes, pp. 467, 486).

17. Commentary on the Words of the Text: Hex. 1, The Creative (ibid., p. 382).

18. Commentary on the Decision: Hex. 49, Revolution: "Heaven and earth bring about revolution, and the four seasons complete themselves thereby." And Hex. 60, Limitation: "Heaven and earth have their order, and the four seasons of the year arise therefrom" (cf. ibid., pp. 636, 695).

19. Ibid., pp. 219, 302.

20. Commentary on the Decision: Hex. 32, Duration (ibid., p. 546).

Time in its relation to the formative process is then discussed in detail in the Commentary on the Decision, Hexagram 22, *Pi*, Grace: "This is the form of heaven.[21] Having form, clear and still [literally, "capable of holding back"]: this is the form of men. If the form of heaven is contemplated, the changes of time can be discovered. If the forms of men are contemplated, one can shape the world."[22]

Highly illuminating is the passage, also in the Commentary on the Words of the Text, on nine in the fifth place of the first hexagram, describing the relation of the great man to heaven (nature) and time: "When he [the great man] acts in advance [*hsien-t'ien*, in the a priori, theoretical sense] of heaven, heaven does not contradict him. When he follows heaven [*hou-t'ien*, in the a posteriori, empirical sense] he adapts himself to the time of heaven [literally, "receives time from heaven"]."[23]

These passages clearly show how the concept of time is naturally conditioned; time retains its inner cohesion amid unremitting change. They also disclose the concrete and formative character of time, the way in which it is in tune with certain situations and induces them.

To be sure, all these quotations are taken from the later strata of the Book of Changes. This concept of time is contained implicitly in the earlier strata, but here the word *time* is used only once and is nowhere explicitly defined.

The only use of the word in the earlier strata occurs in Hexagram 54, *Kuei Mei*, The Marrying Maiden, a hexagram remarkably full of traps and pitfalls:

above Chen	The Arousing, Thunder
below Tui	The Joyous, Lake

21. The sentence relating what the form of heaven is has been lost. Wang Pi fills in "The firm and the yielding unite alternately."
22. Wilhelm-Baynes, p. 495.
23. Ibid., pp. 382–83.

[19]

The Judgment on this situation runs strangely: "Undertakings bring misfortune. Nothing that would further." And the text of the Image runs: "Thus the superior man understands the transitory in the light of the eternity of the end."

The lines of this text also point to many discouraging aspects. The intellectual independence of the authors of this book is evident; they did not formulate their texts in accordance with the requirements of the social institutions of their time, but represented a situation as it actually is, in disregard of the rules of propriety of a given period. The only note of cheer in this hexagram occurs in nine in the fourth place, which deals with the maiden who arrives late at her marriage: "The marrying maiden draws out the allotted time. A late marriage comes in due course [literally, "has its proper time"]." We may congratulate this independent person who does not wish to enter into a marriage merely because it is in keeping with custom, preferring to wait until the "proper time" provides the basis for a real marriage.[24]

To this line text we might add two more Image texts that, though of later date, come very close in their wording to the original situation. The first is Hexagram 25, *Wu Wang*, Innocence:

above	Ch'ien	The Creative, Heaven
below	Chen	The Arousing, Thunder

The Image: "The kings of old nourished all beings, equaling the times in abundance."[25]

This sentence may perhaps be explained by the notion that the

24. Cf. also the Commentary on the Images for this line, and my father's remarks, ibid., p. 667. The Commentary has also been handed down in another version, which might be translated: "Resolved to let slip the allotted time, she will go only when the right time is at hand." As for the meaning of the word *shih*, "time," it is characteristic that here, and in one version of another passage (Hex. 39, Obstruction, Commentary on the Images, six at the beginning), it seems to be interchangeable with the word *tai*, "to wait."

25. Cf. ibid., p. 101.

state of naïve innocence has something two-edged about it, since it can be so easily lost.[26] Thus the Commentary on the Decision says, among other things: "When innocence is gone, where can one go? When the will of heaven does not protect one, can one do anything?" And the commentary known as Miscellaneous Notes on the Hexagrams adds: "Innocence is a catastrophe."[27] For so frail a creature as man it is evidently no easy matter to maintain himself in the unstable situation of innocence. He whose position requires it can apparently only preserve his innocence by abundantly nourishing all beings, the wicked along with the righteous, just as the times in their blindness show no one favor or disfavor.

Another Image text that places the concept of time in a new light may be found in Hexagram 49, *Ko,* Revolution:

☱	*above*	Tui	The Joyous, Lake
☲	*below*	Li	The Clinging, Fire

This hexagram contains many recollections of the rise to power of the Chou dynasty. The hexagram states that it is salutary to change the form of government (nine in the fourth place), and that in such a situation it is not even necessary to wait for the oracle (nine in the fifth place). The Image for this hexagram runs: "Thus the superior man sets the calendar in order and makes the seasons clear."[28]

Here, then, the natural concept of time is coupled with the mathe-

26. This is made particularly clear by the line text on six in the third place, where someone in all innocence filches a cow tethered by someone else also in all innocence. The line text calls this "undeserved misfortune." Here again we see the author free from the bourgeois morality of ownership. It continues: "The wanderer's gain is the citizen's loss" (cf. ibid., p. 102).

27. Cf. ibid., p. 510.

28. There is actually a tradition that the omens were unfavorable when King Wu went into the great battle that gave him command of the empire. Another tradition has it that the tortoise oracle advised against the battle, but that the yarrow stalk oracle was favorable. See ibid., p. 190.

matical-astronomical concept. In this way time can be handed down to the people—that is, a political use can be made of this formative function of natural time.

In the sixty-four situations of the Book of Changes the time element is not always given equal emphasis. Although it is always present and significant, there are situations in which other factors are so dominant that no mention is made of time. But in other situations, the time element is so essential as to determine the total constellation. In these cases the Commentary on the Decision says that the time of a certain situation is great, and it can happen that the situation as such may be great or significant. However, a glance at the hexagrams in question shows that this is not necessarily so, but that these remarks stress the weight of the time category in a situation. We find such a remark in connection with Hexagrams 27, *I*, Nourishment; 28, *Ta Kuo*, Preponderance of the Great; 40, *Hsieh*, Deliverance; and 49, *Ko*, Revolution.

In other instances the Commentary on the Decision stresses a particular aspect of the time concept. Often the meaning of the time of a given situation is called great. The word *I*, here rendered as "meaning," refers not so much to meaning in general as to the normative significance. Here time has the force of a verdict by which certain relations are decided, so that it binds like a law. Such a statement is found in Hexagrams 17, *Sui*, Following; 33, *Tun*, Retreat; 44, *Kou*, Coming to Meet; and 56, *Lü*, The Wanderer—all situations in which, for better or worse, "the father's house has been forsaken."

Then reference is made to the practical effect of time, and this is called great, especially in certain—but not all—unfavorable circumstances, as in Hexagrams 29, *K'an*, The Abysmal, Danger; 38, *K'uei*, Opposition; and 39, *Chien*, Obstruction.

A man's relation to time, understood thus, may be taken as a task or as foreordained destiny. In some situations one can assume a correct or a wrong attitude toward time, while in others one must

accept the time as fate. The most advantageous relation to time is
naturally that of harmony. In the situations where one is in harmony with time, the maxims of action are a matter of course, or
at least they are easy to follow. We have already noted examples
of the man who is within the time or *has* the right time (as though
in his possession). In these cases success comes of itself, or in any
event it is not difficult "to go with time," "to act in keeping with
time," "to act in a timely [*zeitgemäss*] way." The classic example
of these situations is contained in the Commentary on the Words
of the Text, on the second hexagram, K'un, The Receptive: "The
way of the Receptive—how devoted it is! It receives heaven into
itself and acts in its own time."[29]

Equally simple is the situation in the cases of Hexagrams 41 and
42, *Sun* and *I*, Decrease and Increase, where the Commentary on
the Decision runs: "In decreasing and increasing, in being full and
being empty, one must go with the time," and "The way of Increase everywhere proceeds in harmony with the time."[30]

Somewhat more personal initiative is required in the case of
Hexagram 14, *Ta Yu*, Possession in Great Measure. This, too, is
a situation blessed by time, but one that can be fully exploited only
by the attitude one assumes. Here the Commentary on the Decision
says: "His character . . . finds correspondence in heaven and moves
with the time; hence the words, 'Supreme success.' "[31]

Even less promising situations can be influenced through their
time element and by a correct timely (*zeitgemäss*) attitude, so
that good fortune, or even great good fortune, may result. This is
the case, for example, in Hexagram 62, *Hsiao Kuo*, Preponderance

29. Ibid., p. 392.

30. Here much is retained of the seasonal character of the word *time*. But
see the preceding passage: " 'Two small bowls' [used for offerings] is in
accord with the time" (literally, "have their right time"). And: "There is a
time for decreasing the firm and a time for increasing the yielding." See ibid.,
pp. 590, 597.

31. Ibid., p. 457.

of the Small. Here we have a transitional situation brought about by little things (mortar and pestle); the situation is characterized as follows in the Judgment: "The flying bird brings the message: It is not well to strive upward, it is well to remain below. Great good fortune." On this the Commentary on the Decision remarks: "To be furthered in transition by perseverance: this means going with the time."[32]

Even situations that outwardly seem still more unfavorable may be turned to success with the help of the time element, as, for example, in Hexagram 33, *Tun*, Retreat, where the Judgment promises success despite contrary circumstances. The Commentary on the Decision explains this as follows: "The firm is in the appropriate place and finds correspondence. This means that one is in accord with the time."[33]

But to keep in accord with the time often requires greater exertions. Twice Hexagram 1, *Ch'ien*, The Creative, describes a situation in which this harmony can be preserved or induced only if all energies are brought to bear. In nine in the third place, the time of the first action of the creative man, the line text runs: "All day long the superior man is creatively active. At nightfall his mind is still beset with cares. Danger. No blame." On which a passage in the Commentary on the Words of the Text remarks: "All day long he is creatively active in order to act in harmony with the time." These nights beset with worry show a consciousness of responsibility, an awareness that in all such situations even a creative genius can act only in accord with the time.[34]

In the succeeding stage of the same hexagram, the line text runs: "Wavering flight over the depths. No blame." Here the time factor is still extremely significant, and strenuous endeavor is needed to keep step with the time. To be sure, an effort of a different kind is

32. Ibid., p. 705.
33. Ibid., p. 551.
34. Cf. ibid., pp. 380–81.

called for. Whereas nine in the third place called for outward action, here work on oneself is required. On this line the Commentary on the Words of the Text says: "The superior man fosters his character and labors at his task, in order to keep pace with the time." In these two line texts the desired harmony with time is expressed in different ways. In the first case, action must be in tune with an existing harmony with time; in the second case, man requires every effort even to keep pace with the time.[35]

Finally, a remark in the Great Treatise throws light on still another highly dramatic case of timely action. The reference is to six at the top in Hexagram 40, *Hsieh*, Deliverance:

above	Chen	The Arousing, Thunder
below	K'an	The Abysmal, Water

The text runs: "The prince shoots at a hawk on a high wall. He kills it. Everything serves to further." On this archetype of the supreme and ultimate deliverance, the Great Treatise remarks: "The superior man contains the means in his own person. He bides his time and then acts."[36] Here the superior man must await the exact time in which the act of deliverance alone can be effected. "Too early" or "too late" will deflect the arrow from its target (deliverance, not the slaying of the hawk). Having to await the proper time in a tense situation of this sort may be more difficult than the active participation required in the situations of *Ch'ien*, The Creative.

Of course, this harmony with time is not something that is present or can be induced in all cases. The Book of Changes also contains some situations in which it is not possible, or is not attained, because of either fate or a man's own fault. Consider, for example, the tragic six at the beginning of Hexagram 48, *Ching*, The Well:

35. Cf. ibid., p. 381.
36. Ibid., p. 157.

☵ *above* K'an The Abysmal, Water
☴ *below* Sun The Gentle, Wind, Wood

"One does not drink the mud of the well. No animals come to an old well." And the Commentary on the Images: "Time has rejected it." The situation speaks for itself. Suddenly the well's function of supplying life-giving water can no longer be fulfilled. And no personal exertion can do anything about it.[37]

Another situation is perhaps still more tragic, namely, the nine in the second place, again of the first hexagram, where the Creative first appears but cannot rise over the field, hence remains without success and response. Here again the Commentary on the Words of the Text says: "Time has rejected him."[38] Here it is not the exhausted old man, but the creative young man whom time passes by. He must subordinate himself, and it is not given him to rise above the community of men. This situation, too, is the consequence not of his own failure but of fate.[39]

In one case the Commentary on the Images attributes lack of harmony with the time to personal failing and speaks of "missing the time." The underlying situation is to be found in Hexagram 60, *Chieh*, Limitation:

☵ *above* K'an The Abysmal, Water
☱ *below* Tui The Joyous, Lake

This is one of those signs under which inconveniences are overcome with relative ease, or at least borne without great disadvantage,[40] since it is provided that the limitation should be accepted

37. Cf. ibid., p. 632.

38. Cf. ibid., p. 380. My father's translation, "The reason is that he is not needed as yet," is euphemistic.

39. Cf. the passage in *Shih-tzu* (Sun Hsing-yen's ed., *chüan* 2, fragment 174): "The wild duck is called *Fu*, the domestic duck *Wu*. Its wings are unsuited to flying. Like a common man it guards the fields and nothing more."

40. A line in the Commentary on the Decision runs: "Where limitation is applied in the creation of [political] institutions, property is not encroached upon, and people are not harmed" (Wilhelm-Baynes, p. 695).

without bitterness. Only two of the limited, that is, restricted, lines are really unfortunate: six at the top, which carries the restriction beyond necessity to the point of bitterness, and nine in the second place, where the line-text runs: "Not going out of the gate and the courtyard brings misfortune." On this line the Commentary on the Images says: "Such a missing of the [right] time is really the limit!"[41]

Actually, the gate stands open to this line; the line itself is strong and presses for activity. If we still practice limitation here, it looks as if we do not understand the time. But the amusing dissatisfaction of the commentary should not be taken too seriously, for a glance at the sign as a whole shows us what we would come to if we should accede to the urge for motion and gaily pass through the gate: we would come to the abyss. Here the commentary seems guilty of a certain shortsightedness in condemning the man who accepts the drawbacks of restriction in order to avoid being carried away by the vortex of the abyss. From the standpoint of the line's position alone the commentary is right. But here it takes the time in too personal a sense.[42] And many who have succumbed to the lure of an open gate have learned this to their grief.

We have mentioned a number of cases in which time was basic to or formative of the situation of the hexagram as a whole, or played a part in one of its stages. In all these situations time is one element among many. But among the sixty-four hexagrams there is one that, according to the Miscellaneous Notes on the Hexagrams, rests entirely on time. This is Hexagram 26, *Ta Ch'u*, The Taming Power of the Great:

☶	*above* Ken	Keeping Still, Mountain
☰	*below* Ch'ien	The Creative, Heaven

41. Cf. ibid., p. 696.

42. This is clear, too, from the contradiction between the sign's nuclear trigrams: *Chen*, The Arousing, or Movement, whose first line this is, is opposed by *Ken*, Keeping Still.

[27]

The archetypal situation from which this sign starts is the taming of the domestic animals, the ox and the pig—that is, the herd animal and the animal of the lower individualism, which wallows in its own muck. Untamed, both animals signify a danger to life and limb; tamed, they are extremely useful and indispensable aids in the building of material civilization. The ox draws the plow and pulls loads, the pig fertilizes the fields and serves for food.

The danger presented by these animals running around untamed is clearly expressed in the first three strong lines of the sign. Awareness of the danger (fear) is so great as to encourage "armed defense." However, despite all their masculine power it is not given to any of the three yang lines to exorcise the danger and tame the animals. They find it advantageous to stand aside. They even fall into situations of helplessness (the axletrees are taken from the wagon), or prefer to seek an escape. It is the two yin lines in the fourth and fifth place that accomplish the task of taming. The way in which they do this varies. To take his wildness from the bull is relatively easy; one acts even before the wildness appears. A headboard attached to the young bull keeps his horns from growing dangerously. With the boar, a stronger kind of intervention is necessary; gelding deprives the boar of his savagery (that is, his nature is changed). Both operations are wholly successful solely because of their timeliness, and thus make room for nine at the top, the way of heaven,[43] the time when again "truth works in the great":

"The way of the Receptive—how successful it is! It receives heaven into itself and acts in accord with its own time."

43. Here "way" is not *tao* but the path of natural development.

II

THE CREATIVE PRINCIPLE

I

Anyone who has had dealings with the intellectual world of classical China must have been struck by the small role that mythology plays there. Classical China knows no real myths. This is true of the elevated literature in which the earliest writings, unlike those of other cultures, have an historical, poetic, philosophic, and sociological content. It is also true of the folklore, despite its wealth of fairy tales and legends. Whatever preclassical China may have had in the way of myths has been destroyed or reinterpreted beyond recognition. A few of these myths can still be reconstructed from bits that are left in various traditions, as perhaps the myth of Kun, who stole a clod of earth from heaven to stop the flood waters and, for this reason, fell forfeit to death. His son Yü, who was cut from his dead body with the *wu*-knife, became the conqueror of the flood, although at the same time he was the great water monster.

The myths that do still exist play a very different part here than in other cultures; they occupy a different place in the intellectual structure. The P'an-ku myth, which appears to have all the attributes of a cosmogonic myth, may serve as an example. P'an-ku is usually represented as a dwarfish figure, clothed in a bearskin or an apron of leaves, provided often with two horns, and holding a hammer and chisel in his hands. He is said to have chiseled the world out of chaos, a labor requiring eighteen thousand years. Finally he died in order to give his work life: from his head came the mountains; from his breath, wind and clouds; from his voice, the thunder; from his limbs, the four quarters of the world; from his blood, the rivers; from his flesh, the soil; from his beard, the constellations; from skin and hair, plants and trees; from teeth, bones, and bone marrow, the metals and precious stones; from his sweat, the rain; and from his fleas and lice—men. It can be shown, however, that this myth was late and not of Chinese origin and—still more important—that it played a very minor part in Chinese intellectual life. It was recounted as a fairy tale, not as a sacred event, and never radiated the compelling strength that emanates from truly sacred myths. Unlike other myths, it did not work formatively upon the spirit of the time and did not call it into being. It was a myth without renewal.

Beneath the surface of the classical world, but alongside it, much that can be explained as the precipitate of early myths has been preserved in the popular religious rites and rituals and also in daily life. Tales that often look like myths have collected around certain customs and usages. Yet these tales seem rather to be reflections upon the custom or the usage and hence to be constructs or reconstructions; although they mirror in a way the original source, it seems as if they have strength to carry on the custom or prop up the tabu, but not enough to serve as models for the production of something new.

And this is not accidental. The classical Chinese world is not like the Greek or Indian world in which mythology plays such a significant role. Yet the creators of the classical Chinese world were not unfamiliar with what emerges from darkness. Like the long-legged fly in Yeats's poem,[1] they hovered upon the stream, and

1. William Butler Yeats, "Long Legged Fly" in *The Collected Poems of*

their spirit moved upon silence. They did not disregard, reinter-pret, or, above all, suppress the voices of silence that they per-ceived. However, it was clear to them that the dark door may lead to either a heaven or a hell, and that every power emerging from it may take either heavenly or hellish forms. From this the insight developed that a clarification was needed, and an ordering, if these forces were to be creative and not ruinous.

The Book of Changes is an attempt to do justice to this insight. It is an attempt to come nearer to the same universal problems whose reflection in other cultures has led to the insights expressed in their various mythologies; in particular, it is an attempt to come near to a solution for the ever-present problem of duration and change, of being and becoming. The way in which the authors of the Book of Changes grasped these problems can be conceived—although admittedly this is a great simplification—as the reverse of the view that other peoples have contributed to the subject. Apparently to the Indians and to the early Greeks, the created world in itself appeared static, at rest, lasting. The forces breaking into it, changing its lastingness into motion, creating the new, and pointing the way to constant renewal were expressed as myths, and these have in their very nature something that is shattering, repugnant to order, and consequently inherently tragic. The ten-sion between myths like these and the unchangingness of the world is therefore so strong that they do not serve for a single act of re-newal only, but inaugurate a trend of future renewals, even of regular motions.[2] They are formulations of primordial images (archetypes), which, once joined to consciousness, lose their ef-fectiveness only with the disorganization of consciousness. The myth of the fall of man, the Promethean myth and the Faustian, are

---

William Butler Yeats, Definitive Ed. (New York: Macmillan Co., 1956), pp. 327–28.

2. Mircea Eliade, *The Myth of the Eternal Return*, trans. Willard R. Trask. Bollingen Series, no. 46 (New York: Pantheon Books, 1954).

constantly recurrent irruptions in a statically ordered world: Vishnu is not a unique historical figure, but a constantly recurring one.

By comparison, the world in itself lacks duration and order for the authors of the Book of Changes. It is an interplay of fermenting forces, which in their confused diversity stand opposed to order and duration; it is a world of undirected dynamism, a world of chaotic change. Their questions, therefore, are not concerned with introducing anything new, but with taming the existent. Creative outlaws and tragic heroes could have no meaning for them. In this world of unordered changes, the tensions do not build up myths, but primal images as centers of gravity around which order may be brought into chaos.

The authors of the Book of Changes did not limit themselves to setting up single images, they went way beyond that and made a system of such images. In this system the images represent fixed values. Definite situations are isolated (abstracted) from chaos, definite values are allotted to them, and thereby they are endowed with duration. In chaos (i.e., in the real world) a given situation, sometimes an historical one, will be perceived as an image; it will be formulated (imagined), and a fixed value inherent in it will be established (adjudged), whereby it is confirmed as a pillar of order. This system of images linked to values lacks hierarchy, to be sure. No order of ranking the values is set up here, but rather a distribution of values is made to the various situations portrayed, which in themselves are equal to one another. In this way the system preserves a freedom and lack of bias despite its logical self-containedness.

The logic of the system is due to the logic of numbers, for numbers and combinations of numbers determine the situations and the relations between them. A system determined by numbers might at first seem rational and abstract to us and not a suitable tool for grasping the confused diversity of the world. However, the

[32]

recognition that numbers are not rational concepts only is not alien to our culture either. Leibniz was most deeply convinced of the strong symbolism of numbers, and more recent mathematicians, too, speak of the mathematical beauty, the numerical harmony, and the magic power that proceeds from a happy arrangement of numbers.[3] So we, too, have to admit that numbers may help to bring order into the human cosmos.

In the system of images of the Book of Changes an attempt is made to circumscribe the human cosmos. That the world as such was not thereby exhausted was always known to the authors. Nevertheless, it is an attempt to represent the human cosmos in its entirety, with no separation between the dark part and the light, the rational part and the metarational.

In the Great Treatise on the Book of Changes the significance of the images is differently explained. In one section we find:

> The Master said: "Writing cannot express words completely. Words cannot express thoughts completely."
> "Are we then unable to see the thoughts of the sages?"
> The Master said: "The holy sages set up the images in order to express their thoughts completely. . . ."[4]

The images would thus serve as more perfect expressions of thought than speech or writing. They are set up by the holy sages, not arbitrarily invented. How this came about is spoken of in another section of the Great Treatise:

> Therefore, with respect to the Images: The holy sages were able to survey all the confused diversities under heaven [literally, "they had something with which they were able to survey," etc.]. They observed

3. Henri Poincaré, "Le raisonnement mathématique," in *Science et Méthode* (Paris, 1908); B. H. Hardy, *A Mathematician's Apology* (Cambridge: At the University Press, 1941).

4. Wilhelm-Baynes, p. 322.

their forms and appearances, and represented things and their appropriateness. These were called the Images.[5]

Much in this passage is significant. First, it is important that this ability to apprehend should be reserved to the holy sages, who alone are in a position to survey things and make representations of their real forms. The word here rendered as "form" has a double meaning in Chinese, signifying "the formed" and also "the forming." Thus *form* is also a matrix from which reproductions can be made. It is thought of here as something that not only lends duration to a glimpsed perception but also gives it a quality calling for reproduction.

Further, it is important that the representation should be appropriate. The word appropriate is expressive of the right place and the right function. Thus in the representations that the images afford we have not only models to reproduce, but reproducing them guarantees that one is working according to a right standard.

In this way the images became established as orienting coordinates for events and actions. The Book of Changes consists of sixty-four such images, the sixty-four hexagrams. The original system of sixty-four was then reduced in the attempt to abstract generally valid points of view from the sixty-four images. The eight so-called trigrams are certainly of later origin than the hexagrams; nevertheless, they represent a valid abstraction, a productive simplification of the known facts, and not an arbitrary game of the intellect. Both series, the sixty-four as well as the eight, were, for that matter, called signs (*kua*) in the later strata of the Book of Changes, so that now and then it is difficult to be sure whether the original image is meant or the abstraction.

The formative strength of the images is made very clear in another place in the Great Treatise. This section, which derives the creative acts of the culture heroes from the images given in

5. See ibid., p. 324. My translation differs a little.

the system of the Book of Changes, begins with the following introduction:

> When in early antiquity Pao Hsi ruled the world, he looked upward and contemplated the images in the heavens; he looked downward and contemplated the patterns on earth. He contemplated the markings of birds and beasts and the adaptations to the regions. He proceeded directly from himself and indirectly from objects. Thus he invented [was the first to make] the eight trigrams in order to enter into connection with the virtues of the light of the gods and to regulate the conditions of all beings.[6]

Subsequently it is shown how certain cultural creations are derived from certain hexagrams: nets and weir baskets for hunting and catching fish; the market as a place for the exchange of wares, clothing, boats, and oars; the taming of oxen and horses; double gates and night watchmen to guard against robbers; the pestle and the mortar; the bow and the arrow; the house; the right manner of burial in inner and outer coffins; and finally writing as a means of governing.

We have already mentioned the sages' ability to survey the confused diversity of all things under heaven. This ability is defined in another part of the Great Treatise, where it is said: "As that which completes the primal images, it is called the Creative; as that which imitates them, it is called the Receptive."[7]

II

And so we come to the Creative. The word *ch'ien*, which is here translated as "Creative," is a source of difficulties. It actually occurs in this pregnant meaning only in the first hexagram of the Book of Changes and in the writings and commentaries that derive directly from the first hexagram. Elsewhere the word in this meaning is unknown in the whole of Chinese literature. Yet pronounced as

6. Ibid., pp. 328–29.
7. Ibid., p. 300.

[35]

kan and meaning "dry," it is one of the most familiar words and was among those used in the earliest layers of the Book of Changes. And it should be noted that dryness in China has always been symbolic of masculinity.

In order to come closer to the meaning of the word *ch'ien*, in this unique sense, it may be helpful to take a look at its sign, whose primary element seems to be the radical 62, signifying a flagstaff. In the old writings it is represented by a planted halberd with a yak's tail fluttering from it. This was the symbol of commanding power in the army. To this primary element two further meanings are added. One is the word for sun, not the sun as a heavenly body but as a giver of light, a word that is also to be found in the sign of yang, one of the two first principles in old Chinese philosophy. And the second significant addition is the sign for water.[8] So we have here two contradictory meanings: the sun, which has always been conceived of as symbolizing the masculine, and water, as symbolizing the feminine. Thus we find a remarkable ambivalence inherent in the sign, so that nothing human is alien to it (*nil humani alienum*).

The translation of the word *ch'ien* as "Creative" is based on Chinese tradition. The early commentaries that are partly incorporated into the later layers of the Book of Changes seem to affirm this rendering. Again and again we find such sentences as: "Ch'ien begins everything" or "Ch'ien completes the great beginning." And, as we saw, it is the Creative that creates the primal images, although the Receptive is required to reproduce them.

The twofold character of a creative event in which something else must be added to the ability to create in order to perfect the thing being created is expressed in several variations in the Book of Changes. In one place it says: "The Creative knows the

8. I am grateful to my colleague Erwin Reifler for his help in analyzing this sign.

great beginnings. The Receptive completes the finished things."[9]

The creative process is therefore divided here into a perceptive and a formative aspect, where the term *perceive*[10] should not be understood in a rational, cognitive sense but as insight gained. What is allotted to the creative ability is insight into "the great beginnings," that is, those primal images whose establishment germinates process.

The division of the creative process into two aspects is an idea frequently found in early Chinese writings. It is also found in Taoism, namely in the well-known opening of the *Tao-te-ching*, ascribed to Lao-tse:

> The Tao that can be told of is not the eternal Tao;
> The name that can be named is not the eternal name.
> The Nameless is the origin of Heaven and Earth;
> The Named is the mother of all things.
>
> Therefore let there always be non-being, so we may see the subtlety,
> And let there always be being, so we may see their outcome.
> The two are the same,
> But after they are produced, they have different names.
> They both may be called deep and profound.
> Deeper and more profound,
> The door to all subtleties![11]

Here also we have a twofoldness; the perception of the mysterious beginning from "non-being" and the outcome[12] imposed by

9. Wilhelm-Baynes, p. 285.

10. The "know" in the quote above.

11. Wing-tsit Chan, trans., *The Way of Lao Tzu* (Indianapolis, Ind.: Bobbs-Merrill, 1963), p. 97. This is, of course, a much-discussed passage; see Chan's notes and comments, pp. 97–101. See further Arthur Waley's translation and paraphrase in *The Way and Its Power* (London: G. Allen & Unwin, 1942), pp. 141–42, and D. C. Lau's translation in *Lao Tzu Tao Te Ching* (Baltimore, Md.: Penguin Books, 1963), p. 57.

12. Lau: "manifestations."

being, the (creative) "mother of all things." In order for creation by perception to take form, it has to be completed by that which Taoism calls the mother of all things and the Book of Changes calls the Receptive.

The cooperation of the Creative and Receptive in the Book of Changes is often so close that both act together like a single concept. For example, in another part of the Great Treatise it is said:

> The Creative and the Receptive are the real secret of the Changes. Inasmuch as the Creative and the Receptive present themselves as complete, the changes between them are also posited. If the Creative and the Receptive were destroyed, there would be nothing by which the changes could be perceived. If there were no more changes to be seen, the effects of the Creative and the Receptive would also gradually cease.[13]

Already in the early layers of the Book of Changes, and with even more clarity in the later layers, a great number of attributes are mentioned that belong to the Creative principle. One of these, which is constantly associated with the Creative, is firmness, the strong, the decisive, the hard, the unbending. Firmness, which cannot be turned from its way, is above all related to an attitude of will, and the importance of the will in the creative process is referred to constantly.

A number of other attributes are also enumerated, some of which are hard to interpret. The Creative is designated as round. It is designated as jade and as metal, again as the hard, the firm, the clear, even the cold. It is referred to as frigidity and as ice. As a color it is deep red. Furthermore, a series of animals were assigned to it, particularly different kinds of horses, not only a good horse but also an old horse, a lean horse, and an especially wild kind of horse with saw-teeth that could even eat a tiger. In the vegetable kingdom its symbol is tree fruit.

More important than these are a number of further appearances by which the Creative is understood. The father naturally plays a

13. Wilhelm-Baynes, pp. 322–23.

large part, but also the prince and, finally, heaven. The equating of the Creative with heaven is so frequent and so important as an elementary constituent in the concept of creativity that the word *ch'ien* is frequently simply translated as "heaven." [14]

Through the inclusion of the heavenly in the concept of creativity, something truly significant happens to heaven. It is drawn down out of its heights into the human cosmos, it becomes part of the human cosmos. The divine heaven becomes a human heaven. The idea of a divine heaven is also known in the Book of Changes, but the places where only the divine heaven is meant are so clear and stand in such a lively and fruitful contrast to those signifying the human heaven that the interplay of meaning is easily recognizable.

There is a final eerie characteristic of the Creative. In one place the manifestation of God in human life is spoken of, and it is shown how God's different acts are expressed in the eight primal images. What He does in the sign of the Creative is to "battle." "God does battle in the sign of the Creative."

This sentence acquires special significance when related to the idea of tension existing between the divine heaven and the human heaven. For God's battling can naturally be of two sorts. It can be interpreted as the battle of a jealous God wishing to reserve creation for himself alone and intolerant of creative power among men. As such, God's battling is expressed in what remains of the early myth about Kun, who was fought by God because he stole the earth clod from heaven. [15]

14. For these images see the different sections of the *Shuo-kua* (Discussion of the Trigrams).

15. Chapter 47 of the *Mo-tzu* contains a passage that is possibly a remnant of early popular traditions about this jealous god. In a discussion between the philosopher Mo Ti (probably second half of 5th century, B.C.) and a fortune-teller, a ditty is referred to that reads:

God kills the green dragon in the East on the days *chia*
    and *i*,

But this battling of God can also be conceived from another point of view; not as the struggle of a jealous God against men, but as the image of his struggle to impose himself among men, as the battle of the divine to penetrate and be effective within the human cosmos. Thus the eerie background of struggle is not taken away in an abstract image of natural creation.

The word for *God*, which is used here, does not occur elsewhere in the Book of Changes and was little used at the time when the Book of Changes originated. It is the word *ti*, and has approximately the same meaning as the Latin *divus*, the divine, which was also used derivatively as a name for a ruler. The concepts of God in preclassical China fluctuated. The earliest ascertainable god image was rendered by the word *t'ien*, meaning heaven. Heaven simply was God and was prayed to as such. This pure and early view of the divine was followed at a later period by the view indicated in the use of the word *ti*, an essentially anthropomorphic concept around which were grouped the ideas that we ordinarily associate with animistic and totemistic religions. *T'ien*, too, was a personal god, but *ti* was even more personal; he was a god who would draw close to man and could be exceedingly awesome. During classical times the two concepts were frequently used interchangeably, the one serving just as well as the other, but at the time when the Book of Changes originated the use of the word *t'ien* preponderated. In those passages, however, where something very concrete is to be expressed about God, *ti* is used, as, for example, in the statement that God battles in the sign of the Creative.

[He kills] the red dragon in the South on the days *ping*
   and *ting*,
[He kills] the white dragon in the West on the days *keng*
   and *hsin*,
[He kills] the black dragon in the North on the days *jen*
   and *kuei*.

(See Yi-pao Mei, *The Ethical and Political Works of Motse* [London: A. Probsthain, 1929], p. 229). This sounds very much like a piece from a popular ballad.

III

As has been seen, within the human cosmos the authors of the Book of Changes divided the creative process into two phases: creative insight and actual creation. The interplay of the respective powers of the Creative and the Receptive makes itself felt in a multiplicity of ways. Only the tension between them is strong enough to call forth from chaos creative changes and thereby to produce our world.

Yet occasionally the Creative moves into a position for which this system does not provide. According to the Book of Changes the Creative always stands opposite the Receptive. In one special situation, however, the Creative is shown by itself. This is described in the first hexagram of the Book, *Ch'ien*.[16] Here is shown in what contexts and under what conditions it must make its way alone.

To the name *Ch'ien* the Judgment text appends four descriptive epithets: sublimity, success, furthering, and perseverance. These four great attributes are not ascribed in the Book of Changes to the Creative only, they also appear in *K'un*, the sign of the Receptive, but with a meaningful addition: "The Receptive brings about sublime success,/Furthering through the perseverance of a mare."[17]

These attributes also appear in Hexagram 3, *Chun*, Difficulty at the Beginning. Here the image is flowing water over thunder, to which the Commentary on the Decision appends: ". . . the firm and the yielding unite for the first time, and the birth is difficult."[18] Concerning the special aspects of this, so to speak, final act in the creation story, we shall have more to say later. The same attributes are found again in Hexagram 17, *Sui*, Following. Here, too, the image shows thunder beneath, but above, the lake is substituted

16. For the texts of this hexagram see Wilhelm-Baynes, pp. 3–10, 369–85.
17. Ibid., p. 11.
18. Ibid., p. 399.

for the flowing water. In this hexagram, as the text explains, a decision is urged as to which of a pair of twins one will follow, the little boy or the strong man, and a resolve to follow the strong man leads to the true and beautiful.[19]

The four attributes are further to be found in Hexagram 19, *Lin*, Approach, which in certain respects is the opposite of the preceding one, and in Hexagram 49, *Ko*, Revolution.

The word here translated as "sublime" really means commencement, beginning, and is still used in that sense today. Very early it had taken on the meaning of that which inspires awe. The second word, *success*, intrinsically means permanence, duration. It means that which has established itself, which possesses constancy and endurance and thereby gives expression to success. The third word, *furthering*, really means profit, advantage, and, in modern financial terms, interest. Finally, the last, *perseverance*, means persisting in the right; it also means chastity, persisting in a state of nature considered to be correct and right.

These four terms are further explained in Hexagram 1, *Ch'ien*, The Creative, and the material associated to it. To the *sublime* is associated the good. "Of all that is good, sublimity is supreme." Humaneness is associated to it and, as a result, the ability to rule. "Because the superior man embodies humaneness, he is able to govern men."

Success, the second word, is characterized as the coming together of all that is beautiful, as the beauty of excellent, valid forms, the forms of works of art, but also of the beautiful forms of social intercourse, of the mores. For under the sway of beautiful forms human unity is brought about. "The superior man . . . is able to unite them through the mores."

The word *furthering* is associated with justice, with what is right and fair, and thereby also with duty, what it is suitable that

19. Ibid., pp. 73–74.

[42]

a man should do. Finally, *perseverance* is consistency; it is fundamental to all actions. Wisdom is connected with it, and the commentary says: "Because he [the superior man] is persevering and
firm, he is able to carry out all actions."

These, then, are the four qualities by which the Creative may
be known when it has to function alone. Through these qualities
relations are laid down, which, even though starting from the
person who is the bearer of the Creative, nevertheless bring the
Creative into immediate contact with the field of creation. For the
field of creation is staked out through the functioning of the good
and the beautiful, the useful and the effectively lasting.

An early gloss on Hexagram 1 recapitulates the four attributes in
the following words:

1. The sublimity of the Creative depends on the fact that it begins
   everything and has success.
2. Furtherance and perseverance: thus it brings about the nature and
   way of all beings.
3. The Creative, by positing the beginning, is able to further the world
   with beauty and utility. Its true greatness lies in the fact that nothing
   is said about the means by which it furthers.

These four qualities, as has been said, are of a universal sort and
are not reserved to the Creative alone; they are, however, necessary to the Creative if it is to function.

The interplay of the creative personality and the creative field
is expressed in the text of the Image, where it is said: "The movement of heaven is full of power. Thus the superior man makes himself strong and untiring."

He strengthens himself and does not give up; a further indica-
tion of the need for a strong creative will.

The six steps are then described by which the creative process
takes place and in which simultaneously the fate of the creative
man is reflected.

The bottom line has a short text: "Hidden dragon. Do not act." The word *hidden*, used here, literally means: submerged under the water, concealed in it, and water, naturally, is the dragon's original element.

Here we come upon the dragon for the first time. It remains the symbol of the Creative throughout the six steps. In the later strata of the text the horse is the animal allotted to the Creative, but in the earlier strata the horse or mare represents the Receptive. Seemingly, in this case, the masculine has been promoted to a position originally reserved for the feminine, while the feminine has gone ahead on its own way.

According to this bottom line the dragon is, for the time being, still hidden beneath the water with the advice: Do not act. At this time the primary need of the creative principle is concentration, the plunging downward into its own depths, whence it is uncertain with what one will emerge, a situation that naturally prohibits any action. Therefore the attempt to act too soon is clearly excluded. If this line were to change, the person acting on it would be represented by Hexagram 44, *Kou*, Coming to Meet. Its image is the maiden who offers herself, and the Judgment given is: ". . . The maiden is powerful. One should not marry such a maiden."[20]

Actually the situation is not funny! A person who feels creative strength within himself is also prompted by the desire to put it into action. Already present here is that active element, which is from start to finish a part of the Creative; yet the danger of premature action is also thoroughly obvious and must be forcibly guarded against: "It must be checked with a brake of bronze. Perseverance brings good fortune. If one lets it take its course, one experiences misfortune. Even a lean pig has it in him to rage around."[21]

In the second line the dragon emerges from the water. The text

20. Ibid., p. 171.
21. Ibid., p. 172.

says: "Dragon appearing in the field. It furthers one to see the great man."[22]

This situation is perhaps even more difficult than the first. Here the man comes forth among his peers with a message, which he has brought from the depths, and naturally he would like to obtain some response to this message. But it is still not the time to act. The dragon is only in the field, and the realm of dragons is in the water or the heavens, not on earth. The insight that has been gained in the course of the creative process is still unshaped, not yet in a valid form, and so not ripe enough to be represented. This is the time to apprentice to a master and to learn through work with the material.

The man who allows himself to be carried away into action at this point is to be seen in Hexagram 13, T'ung Jen, Fellowship with Men. This is a beautiful hexagram in itself, full of fruitful situations; but the man in it is one of a group. The situation depicted is of fellowship among persons who on the whole do not belong with the established order, who are dissatisfied with it, and to whom, therefore, a creative message would be thoroughly welcome. However, the remarkable thing about this hexagram is that ultimate success will not in the end be awarded to these revolutionaries who set themselves apart.

The position of the Creative in this situation shows the danger of stepping out of established ways with a group of like-minded men and playing the revolutionary. He who persists in this will be rejected by his time. The second line of the text of Hexagram 13 says specifically: "Fellowship with men in a clan. Humiliation."[23]

This is, for that matter, one of the phrases that bears witness to the absence of prejudice in the Book of Changes, since it is not bound here by the specific cultural conditions under which it originated; according to those conditions, fellowship of men in a

22. Ibid., p. 8.
23. Ibid., p. 57.

clan was the natural and honored basis of the social structure. But here the fellowship with men in a clan is something humiliating. A man is indicated who would gladly play the leader, but who for the display of his qualities as a leader has only a clan at his disposal, not an army.

With the third line the situation changes: "All day long the superior man is creatively active. At night his mind is beset by cares. Danger. No blame."

Here the Creative begins to take shape, the point has been reached where the change-over from its perceptive to its active aspect takes place. The situation is characterized by the incessant work of creation and the intense anxiety to have the image come into being. Here a man must work consciously on what he has brought from the depths; he must work upon it and polish it in order to find the right shape for what he has to do or say. Now the time of the beginning is close, when it will start to function; this is the top line of the bottom trigram. It is hard for a man to keep in step with this time, to remain in harmony with it, for time here moves fast; only through careful, anxious activity can he stay in position to stay with the message of this line.

Again, this will be clearer if we consider the man who acts here. In this case the sign changes to Hexagram 10, *Lü*, Treading, or Conduct. Here the Judgment reads: "Treading upon the tail of the tiger. It does not bite the man. Success."[24]

This situation is not without danger, as is made clear in the image, which shows the lake below and heaven above. The sign of the lake stands for grace, for charm. So the strong must here be met with charm. This leads easily enough to a person limiting himself to the merely charming, the merely perfect in form, the playfully pretty, and thereby forgetting that precedence is due to the message. Thus here, too, the advice is that it is not yet time for

24. Ibid., p. 44.

action. In exceptional cases action may, however, be necessary, but then one will have to take on the danger it entails consciously. In Hexagram 10 the words for this line are: "He treads on the tail of the tiger. The tiger bites the man. Misfortune. Thus does a warrior act on behalf of his great prince."[25]

Thus in certain situations premature action is demanded, action with insufficient means, and then the sacrifice of the person himself must not be avoided. Such is the situation of the warrior.

Then the decision falls to the fourth line of the first hexagram: "Wavering flight over the depths. No blame."

The wavering in this case is a spiritual wavering, a being in doubt; yet the situation requires a decision. This is the first line in the field of the upper trigram; hence, a field in which one may try one's strength. Here the way of the Creative, as one commentary says, is on the point of metamorphosis, "about to transform itself." The word *metamorphosis* means a revolution, a transformation that makes something new out of something old. Such a transformation is the first principle of all creation, cultural as well as artistic. The concept of artistic creation is very broadly understood here, almost all realms of life being thought of as ordered by art—not only those that we call art in a narrower sense, but the entire conduct of living, including such things as the art of taking a walk and the art of taking an afternoon nap. There even exists a treatise on the art of reviling. Every art, through insight, effects a transformation in the product that is created, and such a transformation is demanded here. One has a choice as to how the thing that has to be represented shall be formed. "To waver means that one has freedom of choice."

If this line transforms itself, there results Hexagram 9, *Hsiao Ch'u,* The Taming Power of the Small. The Judgment here is: "Dense clouds, no rain from our western region." The western

25. Ibid., p. 46.

region was the original home of the Chou. But the text of the line under discussion reads: "If you are sincere, blood vanishes and fear gives way."[26]

The word translated here as "sincere" shows a brooding mother bird; thus it points to the inner truth (see Hexagram 61) through which a man does justice to his own essence and remains true to his own vocation. This is the behavior needed to cause the disappearance of what was previously blood and fear.

The fifth line is the ruling of the sign of the Creative: "Flying dragon in the heavens. It furthers one to see the great man."

Here the dragon has raised himself to his own element, he wavers no longer, the decision is taken, he is in heaven and can now be effective. The commentary says: "He stands at the place of Heavenly power." That is to say, it is a place reserved for the heavenly; in this case not human heaven, but divine heaven. When the dragon is there he represents the divine, hence the success of the creation is assured. There are no more inhibitions, no further warnings. Here the creation comes to perfection. By following the inner law, which the four previous lines have indicated, it now fulfills itself freely and without difficulty. In Chinese the product of such a creative act is designated as *shen-p'in*, that is, as a divine product. This is the highest stage of creation possible within the framework of given facts. Added to the powerful picture of the "flying dragon in the heavens," we have an addition: "It furthers one to see the great man." The great man will assure that what is produced remains within the framework of the four creative qualities, that is, it embodies the beautiful, the good, the useful, and the enduring; it does not become a chaotic development, but remains within the framework of the human world. The great man is the wise man who represents human rights as opposed to the creative personality.

When this line changes, there arises Hexagram 14, *Ta Yu*, Pos-

26. Ibid., p. 42.

[48]

session in Great Measure, concerning which the commentary simply says "Supreme success." The image is of fire over heaven, and the text of the Image reads: [The superior man] "obeys the benevolent will of heaven." (That is, he follows it or is in harmony with it.) Once again, this does not mean the human heaven, which the Creative represents, but the divine heaven. The will of heaven that is spoken of here is a divine mandate, a command from heaven. The special line involved makes this clearer: "[His] inner truth is accessible, yet dignified."[27] "Inner truth" was commented on in the previous line, but in this phrase it is shown from both inside and outside. Toward men it is accessible, without any pride, without any laying down of the law or desire to assert superior knowledge; within itself, however, it is dignified, free of tormenting doubt, conscious that it stands in the right place.

All this changes in the next line. The sign should stop here, but unfortunately these are no five-lined hexagrams, and every development leads to its necessary consequence, even when this consequence is frightful. Thus we have in the top line, and therefore at the peak of the creative, the text: "Arrogant dragon will have cause to repent."

The word *arrogant* originally meant nothing more than to rise up, to climb a mountain, or fly high in the air as a bird does, but thereby also to overreach oneself, to presume, to be arrogant. It is an absolutely natural result of the situation that this step should follow. An early commentary remarks: "In harmony with the time, he goes to extremes." Carried away by the success of his creation and by the response among men, for which he has worked, he ventures to go beyond what is posited, and raises himself up to look at things from a perspective that makes the posited look small.

But we should not be disturbed by the moralistic sounding word, *arrogant*. This is a situation that certainly appears arrogant from the point of view of the posited, but in the development of

27. Cf. ibid., p. 62.

the Creative it is entirely logical that a man should not want to fall back when his work is done, that he should not want to give up when continuance seems possible, but would want to create something new, which may destroy the framework of the established.

The man driven to this outcome is depicted in Hexagram 43, *Kuai*, Break-through (Resoluteness), in which all the lines are strong with the exception of the top one. This is a break-through after great tension, a cloudburst, a breaking dam, a sign of greatest danger, but also a sign of the highest potential fruitfulness. It describes an unusual situation, which no one has foreseen and which must immediately be dealt with, but it is also a situation that in the light of the transformation it involves may yet serve to further, a state that is immediately understandable to all who have lived in arid lands. When the dam breaks, fruitful mud is spread across the fields; when the cloud bursts, the level of the ground water is raised for the coming year.

A recognition of the discouraging effect of having to remain within the established framework is expressed in the text of the Image of Hexagram 43: "Thus the superior man . . . refrains from resting on his virtue."

Also, as the last line of the hexagram indicates, the outcome for the person who has brought on this situation is: "No cry [that is, no appeal]. In the end misfortune comes."[28]

Naturally it is not possible to bring such an arrogant situation to a head with only the sacrifice of a person who certainly would have had to be sacrificed anyway; an absolute exhaustion of the Creative is required.

And the unusual and unique act of creation that introduces misfortune at this point in the hexagram of the Creative is, as a rule, not a human task but the task of the divine heaven. A completely different word is used here to mean "creating." It is the word

28. Ibid., p. 170.

tsao, which designates the divine creative function. Creation by the divine is mentioned in a sign that has already been referred to, the sign of Difficulty at the Beginning. There it is said that a difficult birth requires the cooperation of the divine heaven, and the T'uan Commentary adds: "Heaven creates [*tsao*] from chaos and darkness." Otherwise the word *tsao* is used only once in the Book of Changes, in the fifth place of the sign of the Creative (*Ch'ien*), where the creative personality appears as the representative of God. Here the commentary on the Image says: "Thus the superior man creates [*tsao*] order out of confusion."[29]

The creative heaven, the cosmogonic creator, is thus thoroughly familiar to classical China, even though more is said about it in the Taoist than in the Confucian books. Nevertheless, the principle of creativity, the highest potency of the human kind, is what this sign stands for and, rationalistic as Confucius seemed to be, he subordinated himself to this divine heaven. A most beautiful expression of this subordination is to be found in the Analects of Confucius. There he is questioned by his followers about little rituals for the spirits of the hearth and home, whereupon he replies, "No matter. When a man has sinned against heaven there is no one to whom he can pray."[30]

29. Ibid., p. 374. I depart here a little from my father's translation.

30. *Lun-yü* 3.13; see Ezra Pound, trans., *Confucian Analects* (New York: Kasper and Horton, 1952), p. 13.

III

HUMAN EVENTS
AND THEIR MEANING

I

The texts laid down in the Book of Changes deal first of all with the position and role of man in the cosmos. That the book is oracular in nature, claiming the ability both to ascertain man's position in the structure of the world and to provide him with a guide to conduct within his unique historical situation, shows the extent of what we may expect from these texts.

When we speak of man, however, something else is meant within the world image of the Book of Changes, something other than the individual, which our more rational age understands.

In the framework of this world image, so far as it can be gleaned from older text layers, the border between physics and metaphysics has not been set. The book does not yet need to differentiate between sensual perception and intuitive grasp. The limiting of the place of man and of his field of action, to which we have had to accustom ourselves, has not yet occurred. This older concept of man still transcends the individual and includes the impersonal.

This atmosphere of more intimate and direct relationship between man and the world, from which the texts of the Book of Changes proceed, does not imply a presumptuous understanding of man's nature. Cosmic forces that shape fate are open to the insight, though not necessarily the influence, of man. Humility is imposed on man as he seeks to find his place within the interplay of these forces, a place that leaves, as a rule, no room for the titanic. For the most part, natural and divine dispensations determine man's being and actions.

To begin with, we are interested here in the effect of divine dispensations on the human cosmos. The insight that the divine will or the mandate of heaven signifies human fate is common to all Chinese classics. This is expressed in the same way and with the same strength in the older as well as the younger layers of the Book of Changes. The word used, *ming* or *t'ien-ming*, signifies the command of God, through which certain institutions and events are shaped and sanctioned. Such a divine command can be issued to man and impose upon him a certain type of action.[1] Man must take such orders into account as he plans his actions.[2] One must hold to a prescribed course with utmost concentration,[3] and consolidate the command by assuming a correct position.[4] Further divine commands can determine the events through which positive or negative guidelines are set for man. If such guidelines seem contrary, one must nevertheless submit;[5] protection can be denied.[6] Whenever possible, one must follow the will of heaven devotedly.[7]

1. Hex. 12, 9/4: "He who acts at the command [*ming*] of the highest remains without blame" (Wilhelm-Baynes, p. 54).

2. Hex. 35, 6/1, Little Image: "One has not yet received the command [*ming*] of the highest" (cf. ibid., p. 561).

3. Hex. 44, 9/5, Little Image: "The will does not give up what has been ordained [*ming*]" (ibid., p. 612).

4. Hex. 50, Image: "Thus the superior man consolidates his fate [*ming*] by making his position correct" (ibid., p. 194).

5. Hex. 6, 9/4: "One cannot engage in conflict. One turns back and submits to fate [*ming*]" (ibid., p. 30).

6. Hex. 25, T'uan Commentary: "When the will of heaven [*t'ien-ming*] does not protect one, can one do anything?" (ibid., p. 510).

7. Hex. 14, Image: "The superior man ... obeys the benevolent will of

However, even divine command is not an absolute power, and the institutions called into being by divine dispensation possess no permanency. It had become customary to interpret the position of the ruler as resting on divine mandate. Secular authority was thus equated with divine will. But the secular manifestation of this mandate and the institutions connected with it are certainly subject to change, even violent change. The word for revolution means literally "change of mandate." This is discussed in detail in Hexagram 49, *Ko*, Revolution, where, among other things, the nine at the fourth place reads "To change the mandate [*ming*, here: the form of the government] brings good fortune."[8]

But not only are the established institutions denied a permanent position as manifestations of the divine mandate. The Book of Changes at one point speaks of a situation so strong that the will of heaven may be ignored. This is the case in Hexagram 19, *Lin*, Approach, in which four divided lines stand above two undivided lines. At the nine in the second place we read "Joint approach. Good fortune! Everything furthers." The commentary adds: "One need not yield to Fate [*ming*]."[9]

It can be said that in general only sparse use has been made in the Book of Changes of the explanation of events through divine dispensation. The will of God can be perceived only in very specific, well-defined situations. In the other cases the created world is left to develop on its own. An unalterable event, unaffected and unrestricted by human action is found only in exceptional cases and viewed as God-given fate. What I want to call here tentatively an inherent tendency[10] forms, together with di-

---

heaven [*t'ien-ming*]" (cf. ibid., p. 60); Hex 45, T'uan Commentary: ". . . devotion to the command of heaven [*t'ien-ming*]" (ibid., p. 615).

8. Ibid., p. 191.

9. Ibid., p. 483.

10. Entelechy in the Leibnizian sense.

vine dispensation and human action, the great Trinity, which determines events.

The interaction of these three forces throws light on the question of to what extent are historical events unique. The older layers of the Book of Changes quite often allude to historical events. We are no longer in a position to explain, or even to discover, all these allusions. The transmission of historical facts has been too fragmentary. Thus we stand now frequently before unsolved and probably insoluble problems. For example, twice the Book says "Dense clouds; no rain from our western territory."[11] This is very probably an allusion to a situation in a particular year about which we no longer have knowledge. Or when the Book says "The king offers him Mount Ch'i,"[12] or "The king introduces him to the Western Mountain,"[13] we are most likely dealing with the introduction of specific personalities no longer known to us. In these and similar cases, our ignorance might not be crucial, for we do know that Mount Ch'i and the Western Mountain were sacred to places of the Chou, to which meritorious helpers and ministers of the royal house were brought and thereby accepted into the royal clan. The lack of rain in the western territory may also have been a repeated event.

In other cases, however, our ignorance of the historical context does impair our understanding of the text. For instance, when the text is "The prince shoots and hits him who is in the cave,"[14] then a knowledge of this prince and the one in the cave would be helpful. We no longer have this information. In the saying: "He hides weapons in the thicket;/He climbs the high hill in front of it. For

11. Hex. 9, Judgment (Wilhelm-Baynes, p. 40) and Hex. 62, 6/5 (ibid., p. 243).
12. Hex. 46, 6/4 (ibid., p. 180).
13. Hex. 17, 6/6 (ibid., p. 74).
14. Hex. 62, 6/5 (ibid., p. 243).

three years he does not rise up,"[15] we would like to know who does all this. A knowledge of the historical facts would without doubt be very helpful in explaining the following statements as well: "Bound with cords and ropes,/Shut in between thorn-hedged prison walls;/For three years one does not find the way,"[16] or: "Darkening of the light during the hunt in the South. Their great leader is captured."[17]

There do exist allusions in the Book of Changes whose historical backgrounds are clearer. Such is the case with the Judgment to Hexagram 35, Chin, Progress: "The Prince of K'ang is honored with horses in great numbers. In a single day he is granted audience three times."[18]

The later commentatory literature did not recognize the word K'ang as a name, explaining it instead literally, hence the translation "the powerful prince." The Prince of K'ang is, however, a well-known historical personality. His name was Feng, he was a relative of the House of Chou, and often called "Uncle K'ang." He was the first to receive a fief in K'ang, acquiring it even before the usurpation of power by the Chou. After their takeover, he received the fief Wei. He must have been in a towering position in his own time. He was later taken into the temple of the ancestors of the Chou.[19] There is also a chapter of the Book of Documents dealing with him.[20] Unfortunately, little is known of his biography, leaving us unable to grasp fully the significance of his first en-

15. Hex. 13, 9/3 (ibid., p. 58).

16. Hex. 29, 6/6 (ibid., p. 118). It has been surmised that this was King Wen.

17. Hex. 36, 9/3. A later surmise that this was King Wu cannot be reconciled with King Wu's advance toward the east and not toward the south.

18. Cf. ibid., p. 136.

19. Kuo-yü, Ssu-pu ts'ung-k'an ed., p. 4v.

20. See James Legge, The Chinese Classics (London, 1865), 3:331–98. On problems of chronology, compare Max Loehr, "Bronzetexte der Chou-Zeit" 1 (2), in Monumenta Serica 11 (1946):275–81.

fiefment. We are equally unable to explain other obvious historical allusions in this hexagram.[21] We can at best surmise that the institutional innovation that began with him brought about a greater security in personal relationships, which was considered progress.[22]

Prince Chi, mentioned in the six at the fifth place of Hexagram 36, *Ming J*, Darkening of the Light, is another well-known personality.[23] He was a prince of the house of Shang, and too much opposed to the conditions under the last rulers of that house not to attract suspicion. To escape persecution, he "darkened his light," tattooing his body and pretending to be demented.[24] After their takeover, the Chou honored him. Legend has it, however, that he refused to cooperate with them as well, finally emigrating with his own people to the northeast.

Finally, we might note the remarkable expedition against the Devil's Land, mentioned twice in the Book of Changes. In the nine at the third place of Hexagram 63, *Chi Chi*, After Completion, we read: "The Illustrious Ancestor disciplines the Devil's Country. After three years he conquers it. Inferior people must not be employed."[25]

And in the nine at the fourth place of Hexagram 64, *Wei Chi*, Before Completion, we later read: "Shock, thus to discipline the Devil's Country. For three years great realms are awarded."[26]

The Illustrious Ancestor is Kao-Tsung, temple name of the Shang ruler Wu-ting, under whom the Shang expanded their ter-

---

21. Such as Hex. 35, 6/2: "He obtains great happiness from his ancestress [royal mother]" (cf. Wilhelm-Baynes, p. 137).

22. It is probable that the Book of Changes originally contained more allusions to this man; see *Tso-chuan*, "Chao 7," trans. Séraphin Couvreur, *Tch'ouen Ts'iou et Tso Tchouan* (Ho Kien fu, 1914), 3:151 (hereafter cited as Couvreur, with volume and page numbers).

23. Wilhelm-Baynes, p. 142.

24. See *Shih-tzu*, Wang Ch'i-p'ei's ed. 2. 45.

25. Wilhelm-Baynes, p. 246.

26. Ibid., p. 251.

ritory. The Devil's Country, Kuei-fang, is the name of a western tribe, possibly affiliated with the Huns.[27] The campaign against the Kuei-fang is recorded, but the details are no longer known. Thus we no longer know whether this campaign was motivated by a desire for more territory, or by the need to pacify a neighbor uncomfortable to the Shang because of his nomadic aggressions.

According to the J ching texts, the preparations for this campaign met with considerable opposition, which could only be assuaged by rich awards (Before Completion). We know too that the campaign itself was long and tiresome, and not without dangerous incidents (After Completion). It is worth mentioning that the Book of Changes deals with two separate phases of this event, the first of which, changed, stands for "Youthful Folly," and the second for "Difficulty at the Beginning."[28]

The later Chou, incidently, seem to have felt a certain solidarity with the Kuei-fang. A song has been transmitted to us, one stanza of which reads:

> King Wên said, "Come!"
> Come, you Yin and Shang!
> You are like grasshoppers, like cicadas,
> Like frizzling water, like boiling soup,
> Little and great you draw near to ruin.
> Men long to walk in right ways,
> But you excite rage in the Middle Kingdom,
> And as far as the land of Kuei [Kuei-fang]."[29]

27. Or the Tibetans?

28. Hex. 3, 6/3: "Whoever hunts deer without the forester only loses his way in the forest. The superior man . . . prefers to desist" (Wilhelm-Baynes, p. 18). Possibly this is another reference to the "inferior people," mentioned in Hex. 63, 6/3. The unguided hunter might have been a self-willed commander who, through his unguided actions, retarded the completion of the campaign.

29. Shih-ching 255.6. The translation is Waley's. See Arthur Waley, The Book of Songs (London: G. Allen & Unwin, 1937), p. 253.

In some cases, recent research has uncovered the tracks of a long-lost story.[30] We find the first of these cases in two texts mentioning the place name "I." The six in the fifth place of Hexagram 34, *Ta Chuang*, The Power of the Great, reads: "Loses the sheep [or the goat] in I. No remorse."[31]

The upper nine of Hexagram 56, *Lü*, The Wanderer, there reads:

> The bird's nest burns up.
> The wanderer laughs at first,
> Then must needs lament and weep.
> He loses his cow in I.
> Misfortune.[32]

The earlier commentatory literature did not recognize the word *I* as a place name, instead understanding it to mean "easy," as "in ease" or "carelessness." That such an interpretation sounds grammatically forced had to be accepted because the historical facts remained unknown. It has since been discovered, however, that the one who lost his sheep and cow, and eventually even his life, in I was King Hai of the Shang.

This king, probably because of his actions, has been excluded from orthodox historical records. The references to him in polite literature were not taken seriously historically, not until the several discoveries of his name on oracle bones incontrovertibly established his historical authenticity.[33]

When all the now available traditions concerning King Hai are combined, they show him to be an unusual figure. Through his reported nomadic wanderings with herds of sheep and cattle,

30. Cf. Ku Chieh-Kang, "Historical Events in the Judgment and Line Texts of the *Book of Changes*" (Chinese), in *Ku-shih pien* 3 (1951):1–69.

31. Wilhelm-Baynes, p. 135.

32. Ibid., p. 219.

33. See Kwang-chih Chang, "A Note on the Days of Sacrifice to Wang Hai and I Yin" (Chinese), in *Bulletin of the Institute of Ethnology*, Academia Sinica, no. 35 (Spring 1973), pp. 111–27.

he introduced a new element into the economic structure of the Shang, whose aristocracy had previously been based essentially on hunting. King Hai is also reported to have harnessed his cattle to wagons, thus increasing the mobility of goods transport. He is called the owner of serving cattle in several instances.

During his wanderings, he entered the country of the Lord of I, north of the Yellow River and approximately southwest of present-day Peking. He seems to have been welcomed hospitably at first, but because of his later irresponsible behavior, he was called to account by the Lord of I. The loss of his sheep may have been the penalty for such behavior, a light penance perhaps in view of the seriousness of his offense (no remorse). That the Lord of I deprived him of his serving cattle as well, however, cut down King Hai's mobility so much that he finally perished.

In the light of these traditions, the two line texts are imbued with new and more pregnant meaning. The six in the fifth place of Hexagram 34 describes a situation in which the power of the great has begun diminishing, but the loss of the sheep can still be borne easily.[34] In the situation described by the upper nine in the fifty-sixth hexagram, however, the wanderer, through his own fault, through the burning of his nest, has fallen into an irretrievable position in which his unthinking cheer is transformed into laments and weeping.[35]

---

34. To be sure, only if external and internal events are in harmony and the understanding of the symbol leads to an understanding of what is symbolized. For someone who represents power and not just force, this is possible only by the resolution to get rid of "goatishness" together with the sheep (or goats). The sheep or goat stands here for the trigram *tui*, which also signifies the concubine. Hex. 43, 9/5 reads: "In dealing with weeds, firm resolution is necessary" (Wilhelm-Baynes, p. 169).

35. The situation is absolutely hopeless and there is no way of saving it, since what has been lost was essential. Cf. Hex. 62, 6/6 (ibid., p. 243). King Hai's death thus does not even have to be mentioned. Both these lines refer

Another historical event, also twice referred to by the Book of Changes, is recorded on oracle bones. This is the story of how the Sovereign I married off his youngest daughter. At the six in the fifth place of Hexagram 11, *T'ai*, Peace, we read: "The sovereign I gives his daughter in marriage. This brings blessing and supreme good fortune."[36]

And at the six in the fifth place of Hexagram 54, *Kuei Mei*, The Marrying Maiden, we later read: "The sovereign I gave his daughter in marriage. The embroidered garments of the princess were not as gorgeous as those of the servingmaid. The moon that is nearly full brings good fortune."[37]

The Sovereign I was the penultimate ruler of the Shang. The annals have very little to say of him, except that under him the decline of the Shang was clearly evident. The marriage of his daughter is not even mentioned in the official annals, but we know now that she was given to a member of the house of Chou. It is very probable that she was married to the Chou King Chi and that she later gave birth to King Wen. That the ruler of a highly cultivated empire gave his daughter in marriage to a barbarian chieftain who was doubtlessly lacking in culture in the eyes of the Shang leads us to assume that we have here an early case of princess diplomacy. The marriage of imperial princesses to barbarian rulers for purposes of pacification occurs quite frequently in Chinese history. The Chou of those times, mightily striving upwards, must have been a most uncomfortable, even an alarming, neighbor. Through this marriage, they were brought closer to the Shang, recognizing and accepting their new responsibilities as a part of the Chinese empire. Peace for both sides resulted. This

---

only to the situation of King Hai and not to the Lord of I, who eventually fell victim to a campaign of revenge by the Shang.

36. Ibid., p. 51.

37. Ibid., pp. 211–12.

new situation brought blessings and good fortune to the Chou as well as to the Shang. The Chou's later assumption of power is not yet anticipated in this line.

If this line changes, however, the result is Hexagram 5, *Hsü*, The Waiting, in which the nine in the fifth place reads: "Waiting at meat and drink. Perseverance brings good fortune."[38]

Through this marriage the future greatness of the Chou became a goal for which they could wait free of care, if only they remained steadfastly true to their aims.

Whereas the six in the fifth place of Hexagram 11 describes the position of the Chou in this situation, the six in the fifth place of Hexagram 54 concerns itself with the position of the bride to be. We know from other sources that the cultural disparity between the Shang and the Chou was large.[39] The Shang princess, now dressed in Chou costumes, must have paled before her handmaidens, attired in the full splendor of Shang garments. The situation, however, is pregnant with future good fortune. The new bride is ordained, after all, to give birth to King Wen, the great culture hero. Her influence is already apparent, her radiance still growing if only she fails to grieve for her past position. The nine in the fifth place of Hexagram 58, *Tui*, The Joyous, which emerges when the six in the fifth place of Hexagram 54 changes, reads: "Brooding devotion to what is in the process of disintegration is dangerous."[40]

Such a treatment of historical events provides an insight into how these events were understood. From this understanding, two guiding principles emerge that are of value to our original question

38. Ibid., p. 27.

39. According to one tradition, King Wen would have been born in a pigsty. See Eduard Erkes, "Das Schwein im alten China," *Monumenta Serica* 7 (1942):76.

40. Cf. Wilhelm-Baynes, p. 226.

concerning the meaning of events. Certain historical manifestations have aspects that transcend the momentary; this alone can justify the building of singular historical occurrences into direction-giving oracle texts. The interplay of forces that determine a historical moment sounds as a single chime. The fascination of this sound is as a rule so absorbing that the separate powers responsible for it are often forgotten. But only by both concentrating on this sound and yielding to it may we recognize its essence and its effect. The mode and effect of these immanent powers can only be understood through their manifestations. In other words, only absorption in the historical moment can lead us to the meaning of events. The authors of the early layers of the Book of Changes seemingly did not make a distinction between immanence and manifestation. The historical moment was not seen only as a means of perceiving or as a guide to immanent powers, but as their perfect representation. This, therefore, was for them singularly the perfect expression of lawfulness. It is in this way that a singular historical event can be direction-giving for recurring events. In the story of King Hai, the loss of his sheep differs from the loss of his cattle. Each has its own particular message, though one did lead to the other. No moment, however beautiful, will tarry, but only by yielding to its beauty may we grasp its meaning. And this is what we need.

The step from the immanent to the permanent, however, still depends on something else. Earlier we spoke of the harmony of external and internal events, and of the coordination between the symbol and the symbolized. This concentration on appearance is also necessary when dealing with man. That which happens to man and that which he makes happen was seemingly understood in the older layers of the Book of Changes as the lighted side of a continuity whose unity was accepted as a premise. This lighted side is garbed in forms that belong to the world of apprehension and of comprehension; images, often historical, alive in the human and also the historical consciousness. The continuity of any situation, however, transcends human consciousness. One cannot deny that concentration on the apprehensible may lead to a distortion of continuity. Hypertrophy of one or another aspect can bring the structure of the whole out of order, and an unimaginative and forced use of the signs creates disturbances that can be significant, even decisive. Whoever does not want to understand the events, choosing rather to contend with them, forfeits his position and his possibilities within those events. Events happen only to man or are brought about by him, and this can be so only because the totality of man comprises the world of events. What we have called external and internal events are really two aspects of the same complex; the flow of events and the position of man inside that flow are the same. To resist this continuity is not to escape it. From this result the words of Daimon: "Thus you must be," in suffering as well as in action.

This unity is unreflectedly assumed in the older layers of the Book of Changes. The later layers are largely concerned with just how Confucius and his school conceived of this unity. We, however, are primarily concerned with the more direct older interpretation. This directness is reflected in a number of early oracles, recorded in historical texts under pre-Confucian dates.[41] In these texts, the historical occurrences are as significant as the advice of the hexagrams applied to these occurrences. While the texts of

41. Use of these texts rests on the premise that we deal here with reliable historical traditions. I don't want to state the reasons here that have moved me to accept this premise. Cf. Li Chien-ch'ih, "Researches into Oracles According to the *Book of Changes* in the *Jso-chuan* and the *Kuo-yü*" (Chinese), in *Ku-shih pien* 3 (1931):171–87, and Hellmut Wilhelm, "I-ching Oracles in the *Jso-chuan* and the *Kuo-yü*," *Journal of the American Oriental Society* 79 (1959):275–80. For a text of the *Jso-chuan*, I quote the one given by S. Couvreur in his *Jch'ouen ts'iou et Jso-tchouan*; for the *Kuo-yü*, the Ssu-pu ts'ung-k'an edition.

the Judgment and the changing lines are often used to explain a situation, the images connected with the hexagrams and trigrams as a whole usually play the greater role.[42]

We may illustrate this with a series of oracles in which the future of members of the nobility, at a time in obscurity, stands in question. The first such instance deals with Pi Wan,[43] descendant of the noble house of a small fief in decline. At the time in question, he was a vassal of the ruler of the great state of Chin. In the second instance, we are concerned with two sons of the Lord of Wei. The younger son was favored by the oracle over his older brother, the customary successor to his father's throne.[44] The final instance refers to the heir apparent to the throne of the state Chin, who was forced to live in exile because of the disorder in his homeland.[45] In all three cases the initial hexagram received was Hexagram 3, *Chun*, Difficulty at the Beginning. In the first two instances, the changing lines yielded Hexagram 8, *Pi*, Holding Together.

	K'an		K'an
	Chen		K'un
Difficulty at the Beginning		Holding Together	

We find the same words in both the Judgment text of the initial hexagram and the text of the bottom nine of the changed hexagram: "It furthers one to invest feudatories."[46]

42. The images connected with the hexagrams in these texts do not occur any more in the present-day Book of Changes. Similar coordinations that are found in the *Tsa-kua* rest on a different tradition. The images of the trigrams coincide, as a rule, with the ones listed in the *Shuo-kua*. At times, however, an older tradition seems to prevail in these texts.

43. *Tso-chuan*, "Min 1," in Couvreur, 1:214.

44. *Tso-chuan*, "Chao 7," ibid., 3:150–52.

45. *Kuo-yü* 10, "Chin-yü 4," pp. 11v–14r. It is interesting that in this case the professional oracle priests all misinterpret the Judgment. An outsider was wise enough to see represented in this text the greatness of Ch'ung-erh's future.

46. Translated "to appoint helpers" in Wilhelm-Baynes, p. 16. On this difference of translation, see my forthcoming little study, "On Investing Feudatories."

The play of images is described in the first case in the following way:

> Chen [the arousing] becomes land [K'un, the earth]; the wagon [Chen] follows the horse [K'un]; the foot [Chen] supports him; the older brother [Chen] precedes him; the mother [K'un] covers for him; the masses [K'un] fall to him.

Although it would be fascinating to follow this shimmering cascade of symbols in hopes of discovering their consistencies, we must deny ourselves this.

In the third case, the changes in the initial hexagram yielded Hexagram 16, Yü, Enthusiasm.

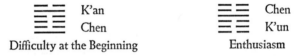

	K'an		Chen
	Chen		K'un
Difficulty at the Beginning		Enthusiasm	

Here the Judgment of the second hexagram also reads: "It furthers one to invest feudatories."

Aside from the Judgment texts, the same exegesis works here as well, especially with the sign symbolism. The exiled successor to the throne, Ch'ung-erh, was to become one of the most famous sovereigns of Old China.

There is another case, interesting, too, because two different oracles refer to the outcome of the same battle between the states of Ch'in and Chin, two of the mightiest in China in the middle of the seventh century. Hsien, the ruler of Chin, had hoped to bind the two states closer together by marrying his daughter to Mu, the ruler of Ch'in. In consulting the oracle, he received Hexagram 54, The Marrying Maiden, which, when changed, resulted in Hexagram 38, K'uei, Opposition.

	Chen		Li
	Tui		Tui
The Marrying Maiden		Opposition	

The exegesis, working with texts of the changing upper lines of both hexagrams[47], advised against the planned marriage, and predicted a battle, disastrous to the Chin, if its advice was disregarded. The Lord Hsien, however, paid no attention to this warning and married his daughter to the Lord of Ch'in. Hui, Hsien's son and successor, was a man of low principles whose acts included incest and betrayal. Through a particularly crass display of ingratitude, he so aroused the contempt of his sister that she persuaded her husband Mu to punish him. Before his attack, Mu also consulted the oracle, receiving Hexagram 18, *Ku*, Work on What Has Been Spoiled. There were no changing lines.[48]

Ken
Sun

Work on What Has Been Spoiled

The exegesis here, working with the Judgment text,[49] predicted a favorable outcome.

Finding himself a captive in Ch'in after losing the battle, Hui of Chin reportedly called out, "If my deceased father had followed the oracle, I wouldn't find myself in this situation." Whereupon a companion explained to him, "The tortoise gives figures, the yarrow gives numbers. When things come into existence [come into the world of appearances], they have their figures [their created form]. Created forms multiply. This multiplication leads to numbers. Your deceased father's deviation from the right path, could that not be calculated with numbers? The oracle was there, he did not follow; what can be added to that?" In the Songs it says:

47. *Tso-chuan*, "Hsi 15," in Couvreur, 1:304—6. The texts quoted in the *Tso-chuan* differ somewhat from the ones in the current edition.

48. *Tso-chuan*, ibid., 1:295—96.

49. The *Tso-chuan* text differs in this case very much from the one in the *I ching*.

The calamities of the people below
Do not come down from Heaven.
They babble and chatter and show hatred behind one's back.
It is simply that the quarrels come from man.[50]

In another situation, based on an ethical conflict, the oracle answered with great precision and incisiveness. At the end of the sixth century, the leading families of the State of Lu, the home state of Confucius, had usurped powers greatly exceeding those lawfully due them. Now the Lord of Chi, the head of one such family, had been careless enough to suffer a falling out with Nan K'uai, the manager of one of his domains. In carrying out his revenge, Nan K'uai planned to overthrow his former lord and to deliver his domain to the Lord of Lu. Nan K'uai hoped to use the Lord of Chi's lack of loyalty to his own advantage. Before setting his plan into motion, Nan K'uai consulted the oracle, receiving Hexagram 2, K'un, The Receptive, which when changed, yielded Hexagram 8, Holding Together.[51]

	K'un		K'an
	K'un		K'un
The Receptive		Holding Together	

The text of the changing line reads: "A yellow undergarment brings supreme good fortune."[52]

Yellow is the color of loyalty; thus Nan K'uai considered this response favorable. He had to be taught, however, that his undertaking would meet with success only if his proclaimed loyalty

50. *Shih-ching* 193, stanza 7. The translation is Bernhard Karlgren's; see *The Book of Odes* (Stockholm: Museum of Far Eastern Antiquities, 1950), p. 139. Even without mentioning the tortoise, the argument would have been the same. At that time divination as a rule used both the tortoise and the yarrow methods.

51. *Tso-chuan*, "Chao 12," in Couvreur, 3:200–203. The *Tso-chuan* texts coincide in this case literally with the ones in the Book of Changes.

52. Wilhelm-Baynes, p. 15.

corresponded to an inner loyalty, represented here by the under-garment. Nan K'uai failed to realize this; his rebellion was un-successful and he was forced to go over with his domain to the State of Ch'i. He succeeded only in contributing to the disorders that befell the State of Lu. This last oracle, more than one hundred years younger than those mentioned earlier, already speaks of a differentiation, in a tone foreign to the earlier texts. Thus is ex-pressed the change-over into that great new era, characterized by the name Confucius. The *Tao-te-ching* describes this change of viewpoint in the following words:

> It was when the Great Way declined
> That human kindness and morality arose;
> It was when intelligence and knowledge appeared
> That the great artifice began;
> It was when the relatives were no longer at peace
> That there was talk of dutiful sons.
> Not until the Fatherland was dark with strife
> Did we hear of loyal officials.[53]

Rarely has the fall of man, the consequences of the recognition of good and evil, been more clearly described. To return after this act of recognition to a seemingly primitive and naïve state, as many Taoists concluded was the proper course, hardly does justice to the complexity of the new situation. Here, too, it does not further one to resist the flow of events; there can be no return to the lost paradise.

Only the acceptance of the existing world as the beginning of a new phase of the story of creation insures and develops the great inheritance. Confucius consciously chose this way. His patience was thin with the Taoists and their occasional obscurantism. When advised by one of them to retreat from the world, he re-plied, "One cannot herd with the birds and the beasts. If I don't

---

53. *Tao-te-ching* 18. The translation follows Arthur Waley, *The Way and Its Power* (London: G. Allen & Unwin, 1934), p. 165.

[69]

want to be together with *this* tribe of man, with whom shall I be together?"[54]

Confucius firmly believed that man now had a new and heavier responsibility within the trinity of forces determining human events. It seemed to him that this responsibility could only be borne in accord with the will of Heaven. Only under divine guidance can the unity of man and of events be insured. Convinced that he too was divinely guided in this mission, Confucius could speak these proud words on falling into danger in K'uang:

> Since King Wen is no more, culture has been entrusted to me. If Heaven wanted to destroy this culture, a latter-day mortal would not have inherited it. If Heaven does not want to destroy this culture, what can the people of K'uang do to me?[55]

II

The word *Way* in the foregoing quotation is the Chinese word *Tao*. In his German translation of the *Tao-te-ching*[56] my father has rendered this word as *Sinn* ("meaning"). In the history of the Chinese language this word has been used in various understandings. The significant element of this word is the head, hence it assumed the meaning to guide or conduct, and, in extension, to pronounce guiding words, to instruct, to exhort, and eventually simply to talk. On the other hand the word assumed the meaning of a road, the great Way that leads securely to a given goal and, following which, one cannot go astray. It is this meaning that has been taken over into philosophy and here became the concept of *Tao* of the Confucians as well as of the Taoists. The later layers

54. *Lun-yü* 18.6. The translation in part follows Arthur Waley, *The Analects of Confucius* (London: G. Allen & Unwin, 1938), p. 220.

55. *Lun-yü* 9.5. See Waley, *Analects*, p. 139. Cf. also *Lun-yü* 7.22 (Waley, p. 127).

56. Richard Wilhelm, trans., *Laotse. Tao Te King: Das Buch des Alten vom Sinn und Leben*, Pocket ed. (Dusseldorf-Cologne: E. Diederichs, 1957).

of the Book of Changes, especially the Great Treatise, make ample use of this concept; it is employed there in a general sense as well as in some specific applications. In addition to the Tao as such, the Great Treatise talks about the Tao of Heaven, the Tao of Earth, and the Tao of Man, the Tao of the male and the Tao of the female, the Tao of the superior man and the Tao of the little man, the Tao of day and the Tao of night. In these specific applications we have generally accepted the translation "Way." For its universal sense my father also uses the word *Sinn* in the Book of Changes.[57]

There is a passage in the Great Treatise that describes how the *I ching* interpretation of the later layers wants this concept to be understood:

> That which lets now the dark, now the light appear is the Tao [*Sinn*]. As continuer, it is good. As completer, it is the essence. The kind man discovers it and calls it kind. The wise man discovers it and calls it wise. The people use it day by day and are not aware of it, for the Tao [*Sinn*] of the superior man is rare. It manifests itself as kindness but conceals its workings. It gives life to all things, but it does not share the anxieties of the holy sage. Its glorious power, its great field of action, are of all things the most sublime. It possesses everything in complete abundance: this is its great field of action. It renews everything daily: this is its glorious power. As begetter of all begetting, it is called change. As that which completes the primal images it is called the Creative; as that which imitates them, it is called the Receptive. In that it serves for exploring the laws of number and thus for knowing the future, it is called revelation. In that it serves to infuse an organic coherence into the changes, it is called the work. That aspect of it which cannot be fathomed in terms of the light and the dark is called spirit.[58]

It has to be stressed that this passage was formulated at a period that inclined toward speculative thinking, a period, furthermore, in which the concept Tao was already a heavily used tool of philoso-

57. For a justification of this translation see ibid., pp. 24–25.
58. Wilhelm-Baynes, pp. 297–301.

phy. The earlier layers of the Book of Changes do not yet talk in such detail about the meaning of appearances and the meaning of events. This meaning is, however, contained within the system, and actually forms its basis. Without such an underlying meaning the system could not exist and the institution of the oracle could not be maintained. As Faust said: "In the beginning there was meaning."[59]

When we now want to approach the essence of this meaning and the possibility of grasping it, it should be recalled that the world of the *I ching* is a world of change. In other words, this meaning is not grasped in stasis but in movement. The meaning consists of the Way (Tao) of change and it can be understood only by treading this Way. In this world of change, meaning appears in grasping and pursuing, in treading the Way, in acting out the meaning.

This solution of the relationship of recognition and action has been treated repeatedly in Chinese philosophy with a variety of answers being offered. The most significant treatment of this problem has come from Wang Shou-jen[60] who, by stressing equally intuition and mundane action, attempted to accomplish a new unity between recognition and action.[61]

In the older layers of the Book of Changes such a problem did not yet exist. The direction (sense) of events signified meaning, and it was grasped by keeping within its course. Progressing on the Way (Tao) was the fulfillment of its meaning.

In this manner the meaning is contained in every one of the sixty-four hexagrams of the Book. It is provided by every event and it may be fulfilled in every possible change of the lines. Two hexagrams might, however, be contemplated for a closer under-

59. See Goethe, *Faust* I, Studierstube.

60. Wang Yang-ming, 1472–1528.

61. See David S. Nivison, "The Problem of Knowledge and Action in Chinese Thought since Wang Yang-ming," in *Studies in Chinese Thought*, ed. Arthur F. Wright (Chicago: University of Chicago Press, 1953), pp. 112–45.

standing of meaning and the process of the fulfillment of meaning. These are the Hexagrams 10, Treading, and 17, Following.

The tenth hexagram[62] consists of the trigrams *Tui* and *Ch'ien*.

Unaffected joyousness, the youngest daughter, stands here underneath the image of the Creative, of Heaven with all its impetus and weight. This opposition of the unaffected girl and creative Heaven is worth examining more closely. Grasping of meaning and fulfillment of meaning result from the interplay of these two extremes among the eight trigrams. *Tui* is the joyous. Among the images that are coordinated with it is the lake, and in extreme cases also the dried-out lake, which leaves a salty crust on the soil. Furthermore it is mouth and tongue, the organs of speech. In addition it is the horned sheep or the goat. It is located in the West, the time of fulfillment and judgment, the time of midautumn when the fruits of trees fall off and break apart, suggesting in extreme cases what is fragile and ready to spoil. The charm of the youngest daughter, however, and her capacity to speak in tongues makes her the sorceress or shamaness. Finally it is stated that the Lord on High gives people joy in the sign of the Joyous.

This trigram is held in place by the Creative, the trigram in which the Lord on High battles people, the cold Heaven, the cutting metal. The range of this extreme tension and the dangers contained in it become immediately evident in these images.

This is expressed in the Judgment text of the tenth hexagram, which reads: "Treading upon the tail of the tiger. It does not bite the man. Success."

Treading, that is the treading of the Way, the grasping and fulfillment of meaning, confronts us here with the tiger.[63] Every act

62. Wilhelm-Baynes, pp. 44–47, 435–40.
63. The white tiger is the animal of the West.

of recognition contains the possibility that the as yet unrecognized struggles against being recognized brings ruin to the one who recognizes. The wild animal, of which we were unconscious before the act of recognition, has made its appearance here. The act of recognition renders him his fang. Once the recognition occurs, it cannot be blotted out. The animal is with us from then on and we have to live with it. Daring and despair of the discoverer are contained in this situation.

The fact that grasping and fulfillment of meaning are combined in one act and that the treading of the Way, the act of grasping and fulfillment of meaning, takes place in unaffected joyousness results in the dangerous animal showing us its more amiable aspect; it does not bite. Recognition (and being recognized in this way) do not lead to expulsion from paradise.

The individual phases and aspects of this act are then treated in the line texts of this hexagram. The nine at the beginning reads: "Simple treading. Progress without blame." The commentary explains: "The progress of simple treading follows solely its own bent." This is still a naïve, unintentional step. Further progress is indicated. The trigram *Li*, the lower nuclear trigram, meaning light (enlightenment) is still ahead.

The nine in the second place says: "Treading a smooth, level course. The perseverance of a dark man brings good fortune."

Here we encounter the meaning. The word *course* is the Tao. The course is smooth and level if one perseveres in it like a dark man. The "dark man" might well be an historical allusion that can no longer be explained. For our purposes it suffices to state that the dark man is not a *vir obscurus* but a *homo teneber*, not one who has been obscured but one who is still at home in the dark world that lies beneath the threshold of recognition, one who has not yet become a *homo sapiens* with his purposes. A change of this line results in Hexagram 25, Innocence or the Unexpected.

The six in the second place reads here: "Not counting on the harvest while plowing, nor on the use of the ground while clearing it."[64] The Joyous has changed here into the Arousing, the lake into the street, the sheep into the galloping horse.

With the following line, however, we get into the web of seductions of recognition. The text says here: "A one-eyed man is able to see, a lame man is able to tread. He treads on the tail of the tiger. The tiger bites the man. Misfortune." Creation through recognition is ahead. The goat tries to master the situation with lowered horns. In this way the act of grasping and fulfillment is only partially accomplished. The seduction is provided by the possibility of seeing with only one eye and of treading even while limping. An incomplete use of the potential can only lead to misfortune. In this critical situation, half the light of recognition and half the power of action will only make the ferocious animal turn around. Half-truths and half measures are still more dangerous than complete abstention from recognition and action.

After this experience induced by premature action, it is clear what one must deal with. One has seen into the eye of the tiger, which up to that point one knew only from the back. Now one has felt its tooth. A new level of consciousness has been provided by the threatening and frightening aspect of this experience. The authors of the earlier layers of the Book of Changes, however, deemed it unrealistic to veil again the image at Sais after this experience.[65] By changing this line the trigram *Tui* becomes the trigram *Ch'ien*, from the west one proceeds to the northwest, the unaffected becomes the Creative. And the hexagram *Lü* changes into the hexa-

64. Cf. Wilhelm-Baynes, p. 512.

65. See the poem of Friedrich Schiller, "Das verschleierte Bild zu Sais," *Sämtliche Werke*, Secular ed. (Stuttgart, 1905), 1:207–10. Schiller's version of this legend is based on a passage in Plutarch, to which Schiller referred repeatedly; e.g., see ibid., 13:54, and *Larousse Encyclopedia of Mythology* (New York: Prometheus Press, 1959), pp. 36–37.

gram *Ch'ien*, where the third line reads: "All day long the superior man is creatively active. At nightfall his mind is still beset with care. Danger. No blame."

In the tenth hexagram the frightening six is thus followed by a cautious nine. The nine in the fourth place reads: "He treads on the tail of the tiger. Caution and circumspection lead ultimately to good fortune."

The indelible trauma of the great fright leads to caution and circumspection, but it does not restrain further progress. The Way leads to more recognitions and more tasks, each dangerous in its own way. It is "inner truth" that brings clarification and good fortune. If this lines changes, Hexagram 61, Inner Truth, results.[66] Blood disappears and fright vanishes. Cautiously one liberates oneself of one's team horse, and in humility one recognizes his pigs and fishes. It is once again the time when the moon is nearly at the full.

Once this attitude is gained, the last break-through can be attempted. The nine in the fifth place reads: "Resolute Treading. Perseverance with awareness of danger."

Here the last veil disappears. The battling Heaven gives way to the radiating sun. This step is brought about by resolute action in the face of known danger. The danger, however, is no longer the tiger. It is no longer that which had been recognized. The danger is rather that by this resolute action an opposition is created between the one who recognizes and that which has been recognized, that the one who recognizes exalts himself beyond the recognized and forgets that with the act of grasping the meaning, its fulfillment is also indispensable. The necessary resoluteness leads with ease to such an opposition; what is opposed should, however, not be considered something dependent. It should be recognized as the clan companion who bites his way through the last wrappings. What mistake could it be to go to him and to unite with him?[67] Once

66. Wilhelm-Baynes, pp. 699–702.
67. Hexagram 38, 6/5, ibid., p. 578.

this threatening opposition is recognized, it can be overcome by persevering in the Way. In such a dominant situation it does not suffice to recognize the tiger, the tiger must be ridden.[68]

As a result no further progress is necessary at the nine at the top. One is at ease to turn around and take an overview of the trodden Way: "Look to your treading and weigh the favorable signs. When everything is fulfilled, supreme good fortune comes."

Rarely do we find at an upper line in the Book of Changes such a measured and contemplative situation. In most cases the line at the top transcends to its misfortune the framework of a given situation. Here, however, appears the opportunity for an overview and a contemplation of the trodden Way. The treading of the Way brought grasping and fulfillment of meaning and favorable signs for the future. Ch'ien changes into Tui, the Creative into the Joyous. A complete circle has been accomplished, joyousness of the end rests on the joyousness of the beginning,[69] a state in which one might want to persevere.[70]

The aspects and phases of the unveiling of meaning can thus be followed in these texts. Within the system of the J ching, "meaning" appears in every given change, theoretically speaking, in the Way that leads from every given hexagram to every one of the others. Frequently the specific meaning of the Way indicated in a given situation is easy to grasp. If, for instance, the words: "When there is hoarfrost underfoot, solid ice is not far off"[71] lead to the Turning Point (Hex. 24), no special contemplation is necessary to see

---

68. Keeping in mind, though, the Chinese proverb saying that he who rides a tiger cannot dismount.

69. See Hexagram 58, Wilhelm-Baynes, pp. 223–26.

70. In a later period this hexagram stands for mores. The grasping of the meaning has led here to formalized institutions that are expected to fulfill it permanently. See Richard Wilhelm, "Der Geist der Kunst nach dem Buch der Wandlungen, 3. Vortrag: Der Geist der Lebenskunst," in *Der Mensch und das Sein* (Jena: E. Diederichs, 1931), pp. 232–45.

71. Hexagram 2, 6/1, Wilhelm-Baynes, p. 13.

the rectilinear meaning of this direction. However, the conditions are not always that simple. The way from Clinging to Wandering, for instance, has the text: "The footprints run crisscross. If one is seriously intent, no blame."[72] In this case the Way is not rectilinear, it goes crisscross. Serious, even reverent, intent is necessary to stay within the Way. The Judgment text of the hexagram Turning Point says: "To and fro goes the Way." The meaning lies here in repetition.[73] The nine at the beginning of the ninth hexagram, the Taming Power of the Small, reads: "Return on the same Way. How could there be blame in this? Good fortune."[74] The meaning here is turning back, retreat.

Confucius is at one point made to say: "The Way of the superior man might be in going out into the world or in staying at home; in being silent or in talking."[75] These words have been said in connection with the nine in the fifth place of Hexagram 13, Fellowship with Men: "Men bound in fellowship first weep and lament, but afterwards they laugh. After great struggle they succeed in meeting."

Looking for the Way and the unveiling of meaning of events will, however, not always proceed in such an original manner as is expressed in the texts of the tenth hexagram. Not everyone has it in himself to tame the wild animal on his own. There is also the possibility of understanding meaning by following. Hexagram 17, Following, in which this Way is described in detail might, to begin with, sound surprising.[76]

> ☱ *Tui*, the Joyous, the youngest sister
> ☳ *Chen*, the Arousing, the eldest brother

72. Hexagram 30, 9/1, ibid., p. 120.
73. The commentary to 9/3 of the first hexagram has a similar text. See ibid., p. 374.
74. Cf. ibid., p. 41.
75. Cf. ibid., p. 305.
76. Ibid., pp. 71–75, 471–75.

We are inclined to see in the attitude of the disciple dangers that involve his personality as well as his way in life. The concept of following here seems to indicate that we get into the position of the one-eyed seer and of the limping treader. The seventeenth hexagram looks at this situation somewhat differently. Following is understood here as the relationship of the oldest brother to the youngest sister, of the thunder that has retreated into the lake, of violent determination to quiet unconcern, of the Arousing, in whose sign the Lord on High comes forth, to the Joyous, in which he gives people joy. The foot, pushing forward, is placed here under the revealing word, the fanatic under the sorceress. Understood in this way, the attitude of following will not, in spite of inherent dangers, damage either part. No blame is involved, and it even has the attributes of the Creative.[77] The attitude rests here on a natural inclination to which one devotes himself. Such relationships are found in the circle around Socrates. Thus, meaning may be realized also in following.

In the line texts of this hexagram it is indicated that the standard, that is to say the institutionally accepted, has been changed or disturbed. These texts also express the dangers that might creep into the situation by these changed standards. The sorceress might become the seductress. The bond of inclination might lead too far into the direction of the little boy and thus the character of the strong man (the knight) might get lost. The nine in the fourth place draws attention to a particularly obvious danger: "Following creates [material] gain. Perseverance brings misfortune. To hold on the meaning [Tao] brings clarification. How could there be blame in this?" The meaning that needs clarification is here also contained in the Way of following.

The nine in the fifth place, the ruler of the hexagram, again calls

---

77. The Judgment text of Hexagram 17 contains the same four words as the Judgment text of Hexagram 1.

to mind a Socratic situation: "Sincere [truthful] in the good. Good fortune."

The word *good* (*chia*) comes very close to the Greek concept of kalokagathia. Fulfillment of meaning in the attitude of following has led here to an ideal that will be served with full devotion.

The six at the top finally shows the peak of fulfillment of meaning through following: "He succeeds him with firm allegiance (even stubbornness), and is still further bound. The king introduces him to the Western Mountain."

Following is continued here unflinchingly to the last. This results in being bound as with shackles. The line does not, however, interpret this as an inhibition of freedom. On the contrary, the shackled one is introduced into the holiest of holies and is placed before the Lord on High. In this ultimate step of initiation he is recognized as a yeoman of god and is accepted into the communion of those who, as patriarchs, are concerned with the fate of mankind. In this context who could deny that the fulfillment of meaning can also be realized through following?

In addition to Treading and Following, the texts of the *I ching* know of a third manner to walk the Way. This is expressed in the word *wang*, which signifies to proceed to a certain place, to move toward a goal. This word is frequently used in the combination *yu-wang*, the place toward which one proceeds, the goal that one walks toward, the haven toward which one steers, the home to which one returns. *Yu yu-wang* would then be to have somewhere to go, to have an aim, to have a place ahead that brings certainty of fulfillment. This pursuing of one's aim again comprises both elements: knowledge and action, the recognition of where the Way goes and the undertakings to reach this goal. My father has therefore translated the term *yu yu-wang* differently, depending on whether the accent is on recognition or on action: "to have somewhere to go" or "to undertake something." The end of the Way sets the task.

Thus, the Judgment text of the second hexagram, the Receptive, reads: "If the superior man undertakes something [*yu yu-wang*] and tries to lead, he goes astray; but if he follows, he finds guidance."[78] Or, the nine in the second place of Hexagram 14 reads: "A big wagon for loading. One may undertake something [*yu yu-wang*]. No blame."[79]

The envisaged aim might be an immediate one or might be concerned with a certain stretch of the Way. The Judgment text of Hexagram 40, Liberation, reads: "If there is no longer any place where one has to go, return brings good fortune. If there is still some place where one has to go [*yu yu-wang*], hastening brings good fortune."[80]

Or the Judgment text of Hexagram 22: "In small matters it is favorable to undertake something [*yu yu-wang*]."[81]

The aim might, however, also be of such long range that the vicissitudes of the day lose importance. The nine at the beginning of Hexagram 36 reads: "Darkening of the light during flight. He lowers his wings. The superior man does not eat for three days on his wanderings. But he has somewhere to go [*yu yu-wang*]."[82]

The recognition of the aim, the consciousness of coming fulfillment, and the undertakings that lead to that aim are, as a rule, furthering. The examples are numerous.[83] It must be kept in mind, however, that the aim is the end of the Way or of a stretch of the Way. Meaning might, however, not always be the end of the Way but the Way as a whole. The pursuing of an aim might thus oc-

78. Wilhelm-Baynes, p. 11.
79. Ibid., p. 61.
80. Cf. ibid., p. 154.
81. Ibid., p. 90.
82. Ibid., p. 140.
83. See Hexagram 24, Judgment; Hexagram 25, 6/2 (but compare also the Judgment text); Hexagram 28, Judgment; Hexagram 32, Judgment; Hexagram 41, Judgment; Hexagram 42, Judgment; Hexagram 43, Judgment; Hexagram 45, Judgment; Hexagram 57, Judgment.

casionally veil rather than open up the recognition of meaning. The Judgment text of Hexagram 3, Difficulty at the Beginning, reads: "Nothing should be undertaken."[84]

The situation excludes the search for the final aim at this juncture. And the six at the beginning of Hexagram 33, Retreat, reads: "At the tail in retreat. This is dangerous. One must not wish to undertake anything."[85]

The situation of the six at the beginning of Hexagram 44, the girl who is too accommodating, is particularly telling. Here the aim has become a purpose.[86] Finally the Judgment text of Hexagram 23, Splitting Apart, should be mentioned. It shows the image of a house that is about to collapse. No further aim is in sight here. Nothing can be done here but to keep still and accept the unavoidable. Meaning is fulfilled here not in action but in suffering.[87]

It has been mentioned above that in the era of Confucius a new intellectual epoch started in China. This epoch is represented in the J ching in the later layers, the so-called Ten Wings. Here the problems of the book are viewed in a new light. The word Tao is a developed concept of which wide use is made. Frequently the word Tao is linked with the word Je. This word probably meant originally a straightforward character, manliness (Latin, virtus) and then a way of acting based thereon, the straightforward following of the Way, the application of meaning in life.[88] The word Je is also used for virtue and in modern Chinese the term Tao-te means ethical.

The later layers apply in addition a different way toward the

84. Wilhelm-Baynes, p. 16.

85. Ibid., p. 130.

86. Cf. ibid., p. 172. "If one lets it take its course" is yu yu-wang.

87. Ibid., p. 94.

88. In Taoist contexts but also frequently in the later layers of the Book of Changes my father has translated this word as Leben ("life"). A justification of this translation is found in Sinn und Leben, pp. 25–26.

meaning of events that does not occur in the older layers. In these cases the term *Yi* is applied.[89]

The semantic development of this word is interesting. It shows in its lower half the word for the first person pronoun. This particular word for ego is used in earlier writings, usually in the position of the direct object and not in the position of the subject. Words of this general class frequently retain the original meaning of this word, which is suffering. It appears that self-consciousness was first gained through suffering rather than through acting.[90] To this element of the suffering or sacrificing ego the word *Yi* adds the element of a balance. It indicates in this way that through suffering or sacrificing an adjustment or leveling is accomplished; more specifically, that through offering a sacrifice a correct relationship is accomplished with supernatural powers. The word then means just this correct relationship, that which ought to be, correctness and justice, and also what ought to be done, what is correct to be done, the duty.[91] The word thus means the judgment of the ego about what ought to be or ought to happen. In this meaning the word is frequently used in middle and late Chou times. In addition the word then signifies meaning or sense. This is derived from the following postulate: to recognize only what is correct or just as something meaningful. Meaning is thus added by human judgment to being and to events. A judgment about what ought to be or ought to happen is an addition of human judgment; it is signification (*Sinngebung*). Here then meaning is seen in oughtness and not in grasping and fulfillment of events and in this way the difference that the new intellectual epoch brought about emerges. The sovereign judgment of man takes its place at the side of his intuition.

89. It should be pointed out that the word romanized *Yi* here has nothing to do with the word J appearing in the Chinese title of the Book of Changes.

90. Compare latin *ego* from *egere* ("to be destitute").

91. Again I am indebted to Erwin Reifler for his help with the analysis of the word.

Within this intellectual development it is, however, important that signification takes its place at the side of the grasping of meaning and does not replace it. Both concepts are used side by side in the later layers of the Book of Changes and at times they are even linked together, as in the saying: "The perfected nature of man, sustaining itself, is the gateway of *Tao* [meaning] and of *Yi* [signification]."[92]

A meaningful order of what ought to be, human justice, is conceived here together with the great Way. *Yi* (signification) can only work when fulfilling the Tao. It has to be pointed out, though, that the intellectual development has led to the paradox that the gateway to this double conception has to be sought in what is accomplished (the perfected nature) and in what has sustenance (duration). In other words, change can be grasped only in a sustained state. Signification functionally works toward creating enduring relationships; it has to concentrate on a state (or something static). This concentration on a state includes the danger that the grasping of meaning that lies in movement becomes neglected, a danger that has not always been avoided. Fortunately the *I ching* has not only been a book for thinkers but also for seekers, and the uncovering of meaning that lies in change has always remained alive.

The later layers of the Book of Changes discourse in some detail on the different aspects of the concept *Yi*. Some of these discourses are found in the *Wen-yen* (Commentary on the Words of Text), of which some parts might even be earlier than Confucius. Here the term *Yi* is discussed in connection with certain attributes of the Creative and the Receptive. What ought to be done has been connected with the squareness of the Receptive. "Squareness means the fulfillment of duty [*Yi*]" it says here, and: "The superior man does his duty [*Yi*] in order to make his outer life square."[93] Square-

92. Cf. Wilhelm-Baynes, p. 303.
93. Ibid., p. 393.

[84]

ness is an attribute of the Receptive at the six in the second place, which is the ruler of the hexagram. It stands for the well-defined field of action within which the Receptive has to keep. The discipline that is demanded by this limitation forms the character; it does not, however, stunt the character. The quote given above continues: "Where seriousness and fulfillment of duty stand firm, character will not become one-sided."

What ought to be, the state of justice, has been connected with the attribute *furthering* of the Creative. It says here: "Furtherance is the harmony of all that is just," and "Because he furthers all beings he brings them into harmony through justice [𝒴i]."[94] Social justice, whose aim is the furthering of all beings, can be accomplished only through a harmonious leveling of all interests. The same idea is also contained in a word of the Great Treatise: "By regulating of goods and by rectification of judgments to restrain man from wrongdoing, that is justice."[95]

The order on which this justice rests is thus the work of man. It is, however, not arbitrary. It is determined by its function of furthering all beings and bringing them into harmony. It is already given by the concept of this order of which the Tao is a precondition. The book *Shuo-kua* (Discussion of the Trigrams) expresses this in the following words: "The Sages put themselves into accord [followed harmoniously] with meaning [𝒯ao] and life [𝒯e] and in conformity with this laid down the order of what is right [𝒴i]."[96] And further, "They determined the Tao of man and called it humaneness and justice [𝒴i]."[97]

By introducing the concept of humaneness the blindfold is taken from the eyes of Justitia. Only in this way can it be avoided that her sharp sword hits the good as well as the wicked. Her scales weigh not only what ought to be or ought to happen and what

94. Ibid., p. 376.
95. Cf. ibid., p. 328.
96. Cf. ibid., p. 262.
97. Cf. ibid., p. 264.

should have been and should have happened; they weigh also the circumstances of this being and happening.[98] The Great Treatise uses the following words to express this idea: "The Well brings about discrimination as to what is right [*Yi*]. Through the Gentle one is able to take special circumstances into account."[99]

The water of the well has to be distributed fairly among its users; the well in this way becomes the center of a social order. The water, gently penetrating, loosens the rigidity of institutionalized principles and takes into account the necessities of the moment.

This relationship between justice and humaneness, between judgment and the weighing of special circumstances, has always been maintained in Chinese social and political philosophy. Only in this relationship can the concept of *Yi* represent the meaning that man establishes within being and happening.

A few examples may show how the word *Yi* is used in the Book of Changes when signifying meaning. A comparatively simple example is contained in the nine in the third place of Hexagram 50: "The handle of the caldron has been changed." The commentary adds: "It has lost its meaning."[100] The handle of the caldron is made by man in order to fulfill a given function. If it is changed so that it can no longer fulfill this function, it has become meaningless and the fat pheasant's meat in the caldron remains uneaten.

In a somewhat wider context we find words like: "That man and woman have their proper places is the great meaning [*Yi*] of Heaven and Earth."[101] And "The marrying of the maiden is the great meaning [*Yi*] of Heaven and Earth."[102]

From the older texts of these two hexagrams we may gather that a naturally given family is not necessarily pure joy and that the

---

98. The word *ch'üan*, "extraordinary circumstances," is also derived from the word "balance."
99. Cf. Wilhelm-Baynes, p. 346.
100. Cf. ibid., p. 644.
101. Cf. ibid., p. 570.
102. Ibid., p. 664.

way of the marrying maiden is full of thorns. The established institutions of family and marriage, however, had to be given a meaning that would transcend temporary and personal difficulties. This is not done by making them sacraments, that is to say, divine dispensations. It is human judgment that assigns to them a meaning through which they will be elevated into an appropriate position within the cosmic order.

The later layers then talk repeatedly about the meaning of a specific situation. Hexagram 5, Waiting, shows a forward pressing Ch'ien, in front of which there is danger:

Naïve action would easily lead into this danger. This can be avoided only by the weighing judgment of man and suggests that in this situation it would be meaningful to wait. Thus the T'uan Commentary says: "Waiting means holding back. Danger lies ahead. Being firm and strong one does not fall into it. The meaning [I] is that one does not become perplexed or bewildered."[103]

A comparable situation can be found at the nine in the fourth place of Hexagram 17, Following, where following leads to material gain. Only moral judgment will recognize that in the position of following, one should not aspire to material gain. Thus the commentary says: "The meaning [I] [of this situation] is unfortunate."[104]

The nine at the beginning of Hexagram 22, Grace, to give a last example, reads: "He [or she] makes his [or her] toes graceful, leaves the carriage and walks." To which the commentary adds: "It would be without meaning [I] to ride."[105]

The justification of this remark is self-evident.

We might once more refer to those passages in which the T'uan

103. Ibid., p. 411.
104. Cf. ibid., p. 474.
105. Cf. ibid., p. 497.

[87]

Commentary talks about the meaning (*I'i*) of time.[106] In those situations when human determination breaks open a given position and forces its will on events, the T'uan Commentary says: "The meaning [*I'i*] of this time is really great." The time that carries and matures such actions is lifted out of the natural development and a great meaning is ascribed to it.

Signification, the ascription of meaning, is seen here in a position equal to that of the grasping of meaning and the fulfillment of meaning. With this, man is given the possibility of playing his role within events firmly and validly. Confucius was well aware of the responsibility included in this possibility. In the last year of his life he felt the call to ascribe meaning to historical events. He rewrote the chronicle of his home state, which was a dry enumeration of facts, and built into it judgments [*I'i*] on temporal events. These judgments have, in later times, generally been accepted as valid for human and political action. For the Chinese, recently awakened to a new level of consciousness, he thereby set course toward unknown goals, to founder or to land.

106. See page 22, above.

IV

THE "OWN CITY"
AS THE STAGE OF FORMATION

I

In the tradition of the early history of the Chou there is an episode whose explanation has always given historians some difficulties.[1] Immediately after the conquest of the Shang Empire we find King Wu of Chou full of anxiety and fear, and in no respect in the mood of a triumphant victor. One of our sources contains the following description:

> When the King had conquered the Empire of Yin and had invested the feudatories, the wise men led the multitude of the Nine Shepherds to appear before the King in the suburb of Yin. Thereupon the King ascended the Hill of Fen and looked toward the capital of the Shang. He sighed deeply and said: "Alas, what a disaster! That I revealed Heaven and followed its mandate took only one day, but its fearfulness will never be forgotten."
>
> Then the King went to the capital of Chou. . . . The whole night he did not sleep. The King's little son reverently reported this to Uncle Tan. Uncle Tan hastened to see the King and said: "For a long time you have been beset by worry and labor, why don't you sleep?"

1. E.g., Otto Franke, *Gechichte des chinesischen Reiches* (Berlin: W. de Gruyter, 1930–52), 1:113–16.

The King replied: "I shall tell you. Alas, oh Tan, that Heaven has not enjoyed sacrifices from the Yin, this is from the time before my birth until today sixty years. . . . Heaven has not enjoyed sacrifices from the Yin and that is why I could accomplish my work today. . . . Alas, I am full of worry and saturated with fear. This is not the time to go into the bedroom. As long as I have not ascertained Heaven's protection, how could I wish to sleep? . . ."

Uncle Tan shed tears over this constant sorrow and could not reply. . . .[2]

In order to ensure himself of the protection of Heaven the King decided then to build a new city in which the sacrifices to Heaven would be valid again, and Tan, the Duke of Chou, was entrusted with the planning and execution of this work. The premier assignment for the duke was to find a new and appropriate place for the temples and altars. He asked the oracle and found this place at a considerable distance from the old capital of Shang, as well as the old capital of the Chou, in the vicinity of Loyang of today. And so the new city was called Lo-i, the City on the River Lo. It has also become known under the name of Tsung-Chou, the ancestral place of the Chou.

What may surprise us is that in the face of political upheavals and political difficulties it was considered appropriate to replace the site of the ancestral temple and thereby the site of the ancestors and the site of the temples. Turning from depravity alone, or a new beginning with an unsullied heart and pure mind, was not sufficient to provide validity again to misused or worn-out temples and altars. A new, correct place had to be found for new, valid temples and altars. And these then formed the life center of a new city. As

2. J Chou-shu, chüan 44 (Pao-ying-t'ang ed. of 1786), chüan 5, pp. 3r-5r. See Bruno Schindler, "Zum 44. Kapitel des Chou-shu," in Jubiläumsband der Deutschen Gesellschaft für Natur- und Völkerkunde Ostasiens (Tokyo, 1933), 2:180.

in the highly built city Jerusalem, it was the holy of holies, not the palace that gave life to a city.[3]

The occurrence described above is not the first of its kind in Chinese history.[4] The dynasty preceding the Chou, the Shang (or Yin), had already counteracted political ruin and threatened breakdown several times by founding a new capital. One of these foundings is described in the Book of Documents. The monarch of that time, leading the Shang out of a crisis, obviously had to fight the conservatism of his people who did not want to leave the old accustomed place. He countered their objections by pointing out that this was the will of Heaven and that the oracle had ordained it:

> When the former kings served, they reverently obeyed the commands of Heaven. But in doing so they did not always have continued tranquility; they did not perpetuate their cities. At present there have been five capitals. If we now do not continue the old practise it means that we do not understand that Heaven will cut off our mandate; how much less shall we be able to follow up the brilliant deeds of former kings! Just as a fallen tree has its new shoots, so Heaven will prolong our mandate in this new city, to continue and renew the former kings' great achievements, and effect tranquility in the four quarters.[5]

In a stanza of the Book of Songs such a Shang capital is described in dazzling colors:

> The city of Shang, carefully laid out,
> It is the center of the four quarters.

3. See Karl Ludwig Schmidt, "Jerusalem als Urbild und Abbild," in *Eranos Jahrbuch 1950* 18 (1951):207–48.

4. See Ssu-ma Ch'ien, *Shih-chi, chüan* 4; Edouard Chavannes, *Les Mémoires Historiques de Se-ma Ts'ien* (Paris: Leroux, 1895–1905), 1:240–43, 247–48.

5. In chap. "P'an-keng." The translation follows Bernhard Karlgren, *The Book of Documents* (Stockholm: Museum of Far Eastern Antiquities, 1950), p. 20.

Majestic is its fame,
Bright is its divine power.
In longevity and peace
It protects us, the descendents.[6]

King Wen, predecessor of King Wu, founded two such cities, Feng and Hao, even before the conquest of the empire.[7] The tradition to found a new city in politically decisive moments was thus already well established.

How the Duke of Chou went about founding the city on the River Lo is described in several chapters of the Book of Documents. One chapter contains a report that the Duke of Chou sent to his nephew, King Ch'eng, successor to (in the meantime deceased) King Wu:

> The Duke of Chou saluted and bowed down his head and said: "I report to you, my son and bright sovereign. Since the King did not dare to settle in the place where Heaven had founded the mandate and fixed the mandate [that is: in the old capital], I have followed the Guardian [his brother, the Duke of Shao] and grandly inspected the Eastern lands in order to found a place where he shall be the people's bright sovereign. On the day *i-mao*, in the morning, I came to Lo. I prognosticated about the region of the Li River north of the Ho; I then prognosticated about the region east of the Ch'ien River and west of the Ch'an River, but the region of Lo was that ordered by the oracle. . . . I have sent messengers to come to the King and to bring a map and to present the oracles . . . may the King at first in accordance with the rites of the Yin make sacrifice in the new city.[8]

And another place chronicles the events following the thorough inspection of the site of the new city by the Duke of Chou:

6. *Shih-ching* 305.5. The translation follows Karlgren, *The Book of Odes* (Stockholm: Museum of Far Eastern Antiquities, 1950), p. 266.
7. *Shih-ching* 244 (Karlgren, *Odes*, p. 198). Much less is known about the foundation of these two cities.
8. "Lo-kao." The translation follows Karlgren, *Documents*, p. 51. See also the beginning of "K'ang-kao," Karlgren, *Documents*, p. 39.

On the third day he sacrificed victims at the suburban altar, namely two oxen, and on the next day he sacrificed to the God of the Soil in the new city, namely one ox, one sheep, and one pig. . . . [He then reported to the King, saying:] "May the King come and take over the work of God on High, and himself manage the government in the center of the land. I, Tan, say: having made the great city he shalt, governing there, be a counterpart to August Heaven. He shall carefully sacrifice to the upper and lower spirits, and from there centrally govern. . . ."[9]

The surprising thing is that the city founded by King Wu's decree was not used as a capital after all.

According to these descriptions, the city that was conceived by King Wu and was actualized by the Duke of Chou was a planned and not a spontaneously grown city, just as all later cities in China were planned cities.[10] Some elements of the pattern of this planning emerge from the quotes given above. It also emerges from the graph of the word *i*, "city." This consists of a circle, an image of the protective enclosure, the wall and the moat, and a kneeling man. The "enclosing circle," to borrow one of Jung's phrases,[11] contains a worshipping human being. The word *city* and the physical plan of a newly built city thus proves to be a symbol of the highest importance, a symbol reaching beyond the threshold and expressing in an image what has been beheld there, the intuitive formulation of a law divined only darkly.

Jung has applied the concept of the mandala to this symbol of the center, surrounded by a furrow, of the temple and the holy district.[12] The tantric mandala is understood as an image of the

9. "Shao-kao," ibid., pp. 48–49.

10. Paul Wheatley, *The Pivot of the Four Corners: A Preliminary Enquiry Into the Origins and Character of the Ancient Chinese City* (Chicago: Aldine, 1971), 602 pp., was not yet available when this essay was written.

11. *The Secret of the Golden Flower* (New York: Harcourt, Brace, 1962), p. 102. Jung's German term is *der hegende Kreis. Hegen* is to protect with love and care.

12. Ibid., Jung's preface. See also Jung's contribution to *Eranos Jahrbuch 1935*, vol. 3 (1936).

city of Heaven.[13] And the Shang called their capital "the Heavenly City."[14] The consciously planned city of the Shang and the early Chou was in structure and function the representation of a psycho-cosmic system; its plan was nothing artificial but was given in the disposition of man. The city was the site of gods and ancestors, an image and symbol of Heaven, as the creators of Chinese culture had envisioned it.

In later ages the Chinese city in its design still remained close to this hierarchic original image. Regional and topographical factors have influenced in details the plan of a city; differences in the functions of a city, which might be an administrative center, a garrison, a center of production or commerce, have had an effect on the overall construction of an individual city image. Generally, however, the layout of a Chinese city is surprisingly uniform; it always remained a representation of the mandala, an image of the heavenly city. Peking, which was for more than a millenium the capital of the empire, may serve as an example. Built on the plains, yet surrounded by a semicircle of protective mountains, it has in the center the palace, the seat of the representative of Heaven on earth, and the possessor of the heavenly mandate. The palace is flanked in the south by the two great sanctuaries that were the symbols of the empire, like scepter and crown with us. In the east stands the Temple of the Ancestors of the Dynasty, and in the west, the Altar of the Soil and the Products of the Soil. Doubly walled, the palace city with its golden yellow roofs, lakes, and parks surrounds a number of other holy sites, among them, in the north, the Altar of Sericulture, the place of meditation on, and sacrifices for, female activities.

North of the palace city the two fabled towers rise up, the Drum

13. Sanskrit: Deva-puri, the city of the Gods. See Erwin Rousselle, "Ein lamaistisches Vajra-Maṇḍala" in *Sinica* 4 (1929) :265–73; Mircea Eliade, *Yoga, Unsterblichkeit und Freiheit* (Zurich, 1960).

14. Book of Documents, chap. "To-shih," Karlgren, *Documents,* p. 56.

Tower and the Bell Tower, protective symbols, marking the rhythm of the day and the year with their sounds and giving the signal for the closing of the gates as a protection against the sinister mysteries of the night. At some distance right and left of these towers we find two great temples again. In the west is the temple of the war gods, Kuan Yü and Yüeh Fei, revered heroes of the third and twelfth century, respectively, who in their defeat rather than in their victories embody the Chinese image of martial virtues. And in the east the temple of the great culture-hero, Confucius, whose cypresses, many hundreds of years old, carry the nests of tens of thousands of Peking crows that, long after the demise of the empire, still show their reverence to Confucius by circling his sanctuary in their evening flight.

On the common outside of the city walls there are a number of further altars: in the south, the three-staged, round Altar of Heaven made of white marble—the "center of the world"—and near it, the temple rotunda, in which the emperor at midnight of each New Year prayed for a good harvest; west of it, the Altar of Agriculture, where the emperor every spring plowed the first furrow; in the north, the square Altar of the Earth; and in the east and west, the altars of the Sun and the Moon.

A secondary circle of legends identified the sanctuaries of Peking and its environment with the parts of the body of the first human being, and the creator of our world, P'an-ku. This circle of legends is probably not old, it may not even be Chinese in origin. But it symbolizes that, even in later ages, the city was looked upon as an artistic and not as an artificial structure, and that, again and again, it was represented in the images of legends most alive at a given time. Beyond that this circle of legends symbolizes the curious insight that the human body is a replica of the heavenly city and that the creator, man, and be it in his death, is an indispensable link in the development from image to representation.

Such a conception of the city imposes special constraints on the city planners and builders. They have to construct the city in a way that corresponds with the original image. It was not by accident that, in our rational age, Hindemith gave this assignment in his children's opera *Wir bauen eine Stadt* (We Build a City) to the youthful fools, who are still in consonance with time and the specific forms required by time.

In the preintellectual period of early China the communication with the sources beyond the threshold was not yet blocked. The city planners have kept somewhat apart from the orthodox tradition throughout China's history and remained closer to the spiritual trends that followed the intuitive rather than the rational. Among their traditional arts it was the art of Feng-shui, the knowledge of wind and water, that was employed to discover the appropriate locality for their constructions. The lore of Feng-shui has often been interpreted as essentially esthetic. That is certainly correct in so far as it taught the builders to fuse their construction with the landscape into an intimate unity; however, the Feng-shui showed not only the beautiful but also the good place for a city. It pointed out the right place at a given time for a given city.

Of the two determinants of place and time, the first is naturally familiar to us, but the second is familiar only in its pragmatic aspects. Functions of cities as determined by time influence everywhere the development of the cities' appearances. In the metropolis this appearance was determined by institutions of inherent durability. For example, the metropolis contained sanctuaries that had worldly functions as well as sacred ones. The feudal lords were obliged to appear at the capital to participate in the great sacrifices, thus giving a powerful expression to the unity of the empire. It then contained the royal palace, whose splendor and size contributed to the representation of the king's position; guest houses for the feudal lords and ambassadors, and later also for the wandering scholars; and factories for court luxuries and the center of national and international trade.

The feudal lords and the high nobility had their seats in cities also and not in strategically located castles or on great estates. These cities were smaller copies of the metropolis, but their sacred aspects were strongly reduced, as the great altars could only be served by the king himself. The tendency existed among the feudal lords to establish particularly splendid ceremonies in their ancestral temples instead, and the reports mention that feudal lords usurped royal ceremonial prerogatives here.

The wall and the moat were also to be omitted in the regional cities of the high nobility and the mesne lords, according to the authoritarian system of the Chou. However, this generally could not be enforced. The archetype of the city demanded the sacred core and the protective wall, and the real appearance of even the regional cities was assimilated to this type in the course of the Chou dynasty.

A third type of the city was still further reduced and consisted essentially of not much more than the protective wall. These were the towns of local importance only where the rural population retired when their agricultural pursuits were finished, and which they left again at the beginning of spring. These two occasions, homecoming as well as departure, were marked by religious folk festivals that now and again assumed a carnivallike character. During the summer, however, not much more than the empty hull remained. This type of a city makes particularly evident the relationship of a city's design to time. In the country it is the recurring seasons, the cyclical course of the year, that is most obvious. Not only could such a rural town easily be left and transplanted whenever required by political or economical conditions, but in a small way we see here the image of a city without permanence, the dying city.

The concept of the dying city can as well be applied to the larger city and even to the metropolis. As mentioned, this was particularly the case under the Shang. Compounds and buildings

[97]

constructed at great expense would have guaranteed a life span of centuries if physically maintained, but they were abandoned without hesitation when it became evident that the city was doomed. The signs from which this death or this coming death was divined were the political and economic situation. The reasons assumed, however, were that the sanctuaries had lost their effectiveness and that the sacrifices offered there were no longer accepted by the gods. Thus the permanence of a city was implicitly restricted by time.

Beginning with Chou times great cities were no longer abandoned or transplanted so easily. The case described earlier of the construction of a new city is unique in the annals of the Chou, and, as has been mentioned, the newly founded city was even then not used as a capital. After the foundation and formation of the new city and after the first sacrifices had been offered, it was left to itself. The city as such continued to exist; it served in the latter part of Chou and in later dynasties occasionally as the capital of the empire. For its builders, however, the fact of its construction was apparently more important than the permanence of its function.

The occurrence of this phenomenon has caused astonishment and head-shaking among the historians of later generations. Before we attempt an interpretation I would like to call to mind a custom that could occasionally be observed in Tibetan monasteries. When a mandala was needed there for a religious ceremony it was fashioned out of many-colored sand. With the greatest of care the priests blew sand out of small metal tubes and so formed an image, which had splendor and effectiveness, out of the least durable of all elements. A careless movement or an uncontrolled breath could destroy the image. And it was left for destruction after it had played its role in a single ceremony.

As we have seen, the founding of the new city was a personal concern of King Wu, one that caused him worrisome, sleepless nights. All accounts agree, however, that the execution followed Shang traditions closely. The site of the city was determined with the help of the Shang oracle, the tortoise, and not with the help of the Chou oracle, the yarrow. It was erected by Shang workers and settled by Shang population. The sacrifices were Chou sacrifices but with the use of Shang rituals. Pragmatic considerations probably made it appear advisable to the Chou leaders not to rule their newly founded empire from the center of a recently subjugated population. Moreover, the capital of the Chou in their own region had just been finished, and their own city with its more familiar surroundings held greater attraction than the Shang capital.

The new world in which the Chou found themselves, and China after the conquest by the Chou, required an act that would again establish access to the sources in a way that would be appropriate for the situation not only of the Chou, but of the empire as well, and that would give this vision symbolic expression at least once. When this symbol was effected, the new city could be left to itself. The shaping of the new empire occurred in their own city.

The suspenseful way in which the Chou regarded their problem and its solution, which consisted in an astonishing interplay of old and new, of the singular and traditional, possibly made them blind to one point: they might have trusted too much in the permanence of their own city. They were to experience the fall of their city to the uprising of feudal lords and the invasion of barbarians. Each, even the most highly symbolic, representation of the prototype transpires in time and is therefore subject to the law of time.

In the early history of the Chou, the dangers of making one's own city the stage of formation also surfaced in this way. They probably put their trust in the hope that "formation," when properly understood, would protect them from these dangers.

The Chinese word for form, *hsing*, does not quite correspond semantically to ours. It is derived from the like-sounding word for a casting mold, or matrix. The Chinese word thus contains a strong normative meaning. Casting results in a product that corresponds to a prototype. Recalling the wealth of forms and the richness of meaning of the early Chinese bronzes that were cast in this manner, it can be seen that *hsing*, "form, formation," means an expression of an archetypally given content in artistic form, a formation that gives to the archetype the directing and guiding force of a law. The word *hsing* is semantically related to the like-sounding word for punishment and concrete law.

Surrounded by one's own city, remaining open to one's archetypes, and carrying on and developing one's own traditions, there seemed to be given a guarantee of possessing a permanent formative power. Formation refers here to everything implicit in man and motivated by him. It refers to the individual personality and the structure of the family, the objects of daily and of solemn use, sacred rites and social customs, and finally to the rule of the empire. In all these facets of human being and human action, formation pressed toward permanence. It was the problem of how to lend permanence to his newly founded reign that caused King Wu sleepless nights. In their own city the early Chou believed, in contrast to King Wu, to have found a guarantee of permanence.

The world image of The Book of Changes is not inclined toward the urge of permanence to the same degree as the rulers of the Chou empire. The world of this book is a changing world; every static expression, every binding form appears here as a frozen image that is opposed to life. The urge toward permanence as an intrinsic part of formation is not foreign to The Book of Changes. The world of appearances, even beautiful appearances, must nevertheless be opposed. This opposition, which reduces appearance to being and form to content, appears to The Book of Changes in no respect as an easy assignment. What needs to be done here is generally in the realm of the extraordinary; it is always a situation of great excitement and often of great personal danger.

So it is not surprising that The Book of Changes also contains a reference to the dying city that must be abandoned. This reference is found in Hexagram 48, *Ching*, The Well. This hexagram follows Hexagram 47, *K'un*, Oppression, which is its reverse. The abandoning of a city following oppression is a situation we have observed several times in the course of the Shang age. The hexagram Oppression shows the lake or irrigation ditch that is drained of water, an empty container without content. The idea of a well thus presents itself spontaneously.

Oppression   The Well

The Judgment of the hexagram The Well says:

The town may be changed, but the well cannot be changed. It neither decreases nor increases. They come and go and draw from the well. If one gets down almost to the water and the rope does not go all the way, or the jug breaks, it brings misfortune.[15]

The well is a common human image of an entry to the origin. Miscellaneous Notes explains: "The well means union."[16] The situation of the text is clear: even the accustomed environment of one's own town, the configuration that once was a representation of a real prototype, the image of the mandala, may be abandoned, possibly must be abandoned, but the connection with the source must continue to exist.

The warning our text adds is surely well chosen: the existence alone of the well is no guarantee of clear insights. Only when one delves deeply enough and taps actual spring water has the well been put into service; too short a rope, a broken jug, are not only without effect, but they bring misfortune. Playing at the entrance to the shadowy depths is as alluring as it is dangerous. The in-

15. Wilhelm-Baynes, p. 185.
16. Ibid., p. 629.

dividual lines allude to such misuses: one may feel tempted to shoot fish at the well instead of drawing water. The well may not only contain pure water but muddy sediments. The drawn water may be left unused. To avoid such temptations and dangers is not simple; if they are avoided then this is a place where life is dispensed with vigor; it is inexhaustible and serves the resident as well as the wanderer. So one may confidently change cities.

Where a too well-defined configuration of the image of the city may lead is shown in a number of texts, in which one's own city has to be punished and fought. One of these is contained in the upper nine of Hexagram 35, *Chin*, Progress or Expansion.[17]

This is the hexagram of Prince K'ang, the younger brother of King Wu.[18] He was among those who changed their own city. Before the conquest of the empire he received the fief K'ang in the west; after the conquest the fief Wei in the east was apportioned to him. This latter region was predominantly settled by Shang people; he thus reigned over a population that lacked the durability of the accustomed and the peace of the traditional. The image of his city was a superimposed one; it might have been copied from the city newly built by the Duke of Chou. The Book of Documents contains a speech the Duke of Chou addressed to his younger brother[19], which reads like the address of an investiture, and in which it is made clear to the prince what kind of a situation he has to manage from his new city. It is strange that in this document the worldly position of the prince is the only subject under discussion. Much is said about subduing revolts and meting out punishments. As an example, his father King Wen is introduced, who also figures here as a great punisher. It is thus a

17. Ibid., pp. 136–39.
18. See pp. 56–57.
19. Chap. "K'ang-kao," Karlgren, *Documents*, pp. 39–43.

particularly artificial, superimposed image of a city in which the application of intelligence and power serves solely the purposes of worldly rule; it is also an indirect, borrowed image in which rule no longer rests on the primordial image but on another example soon to be abandoned. It completely lacks depth, and King Wu's prime concern about the founding of the city on the Lo, the creation of a site for union with the ancestors and harmony with the gods, is here completely disregarded.

And so it is not astonishing that Prince K'ang, after expanding in the beginning, finally gets into the situation of having to use his horns in order to punish his own city. The text of the upper nine reads: "Making progress with the horns is permissible only for the purpose of punishing one's own city. To be conscious of danger brings good fortune. No blame. Perseverance brings humiliation."

Another case in which the own city has to be punished is found in the paradoxical words "modesty that comes to expression." Hexagram 15, Ch'ien, Modesty, contains this phrase twice, once at the six in the second place and once at the upper six.[20]

The word my father, Richard Wilhelm, has translated as "to come to expression" (sich äussern) is actually the cry of birds, especially the rooster's crow, but in addition the cry of the cicada and the bellowing of the stag is so designated. We have here a crowing or bellowing modesty. It is modesty clothed in its natural sound. It is not modesty that gives itself airs or makes a show of itself, but modesty that in its sound, even in a strong sound, still is recognized and perceived directly as modesty, just as the bell is recognized by its sound, a natural and factual self-presentation.

The reason for modesty being especially awarded such self-

20. Wilhelm-Baynes, pp. 65–66.

presentation, and for modesty presenting itself being given the special role of punishing the own city, lies in the place held by modesty in the structure of personality in China. Almost all schools of Chinese ethics, at any rate the Taoistic as well as the Confucian, see in modesty a characteristic valuable as well as effective. It shows the handle of character, say the Appended Judgments. The Commentary to the Decision explains this in the following way:

> Modesty creates success, for it is the way of heaven to shed its influence downward, and to create light and radiance. It is the way of the earth to be lowly and to go upward.
>
> It is the way of heaven to make empty what is full and to give increase to what is modest. It is the way of the earth to change the full and to augment the modest. Spirits and gods bring harm to what is full and prosper what is modest. It is the way of men to hate fullness and to love the modest.
>
> Modesty that is honored spreads radiance. Modesty that is lowly cannot be ignored. This is the end attained by the superior man.[21]

The text to the six at the top in the hexagram says: "Modesty that comes to expression. It is favorable to set armies marching to chastise one's own city and one's country."

The word that is here translated as "to chastise" means to establish a condition of order with force of arms, or to re-establish order. Not every campaign can be described by this word; only those that in the understanding of the contemporary world and of posterity corrected an unfortunate condition. Politically a wide play in meaning has naturally been left here; semantically the word is related to the like-sounding phrases *to make right, to adjust.*

What is supposed to be adjusted here with force is again the own city. It is the naturally modest one in his self-presentation, who does not use his modesty as a pretext to allow through inactivity an unfortunate condition to continue, and who does not blame this condition on external circumstances, but restores right

21. Ibid., p. 462.

where it is most needed, namely, within himself. A manifestation of one's own city that has deviated from the primordial image and has falsified it must be eradicated, by force if necessary. Only then will there be a stage on which formation can take place, on which, as the Judgment expresses it, things can be carried through.

A campaign of a different kind is described in Hexagram 6, *Sung,* Conflict.[22]

Here we are not concerned with a campaign to punish or to set things right, but a struggle arising out of given opposites: the struggle of the middle son against the father who obstructs him; the struggle of one who toils against the creative one; the struggle of the snake against the dragon; the struggle of water against heaven—a hopeless struggle from which neither party can emerge victorious.

The text to the nine in the second place says here: "One cannot engage in conflict; one returns home, gives way. The people of his town, three hundred households, remain free of guilt."

In the context of that age a city of three hundred households was of no particular importance. The intelligent, even cunning, second son must have experienced unendurable obstruction from his father's hand, to have undertaken the struggle against the powerful one from such a narrow base. The insight that this undertaking is hopeless comes to him soon, and he retreats. But he had left his city already; irritated to the utmost he had failed to consider the configuration of his situation. The protective enclosure no longer surrounds him, he has placed himself outside of this circle. To go back to his own city is no longer possible unless he wants to pull it down into ruin with him. The second son is too intelligent not to anticipate these consequences, and so he avoids

22. Ibid., pp. 28–31.

his city and goes into hiding. For himself the obstruction results
in oppression, but the people of his city go without guilt.

We see here the life of a city enjoying a consideration that was
not available to it in the examples given above. In these, the city
was resolutely abandoned; it was punished and chastised, whereas here it is saved. Generally The Book of Changes has little love
for institutions tending toward permanence; and in the two other
places where they are mentioned in the texts of The Book of
Changes, the citizens of a city are teased rather than privileged.[23]
To the authors of the book it was, however, not unknown that
every representation, even of the most dynamic primordial image,
has had a static appearance. As long as this is not opposed to life,
it may and should remain. In this case, where it is not the static
cast of the city, but inner conflicts, that have brought about the
misfortune, where an excess rather than a deficiency of dynamic
exists, the city is saved.

The nine in the third place of Hexagram 46, *Sheng*, Pushing Upward,[24] may have had such a "saved" city in mind. The text here
says:

"One pushes upward into an empty city."

The image of an empty city has something uncanny: an accomplished representation from which life has fled, an empty pattern,
if not a phantom. In the course of the development of pushing upward, this is furthermore an unusual, an unexpected situation.
The image of pushing upward shows the plant pushing up through
the soil: the successful, if laborious ascent. Here now we find in the
course of this ascent a completed pattern that could furnish the
stage for future formation. How should one behave here? Should
one leave the empty city behind, or should one take advantage of

23. Hex. 8, 9/5, ibid., p. 38; Hex. 25, 6/3, ibid., p. 102.
24. Ibid., p. 179.

this unexpectedly favorable condition? One wonders whether one would perhaps burden oneself with a wagon of corpses.[25]

The authors of the line texts have obviously perceived this situation as extremely ambivalent. They did not, as usual, add what would be advisable to do in this situation, or what could be the obvious consequences of this situation.

The authors of the Little Image Commentary have more confidence. They see no reason to doubt, and advise making use of the empty city.[26] It can be demonstrated, however, that the authors of the Little Image Commentary tend now and then toward extreme optimism, that they forget the situation in its entirety in their concern over the seemingly favorable aspects of the immediate moment.[27] It seems to me that with the right attitude, taking justified doubts into consideration, the empty city might just as well be made of use. A self-erected city would hardly be distinguishable in its pattern from the one discovered. The doubts should protect one, however, from taking on the phantoms of the past with the pattern.

II

In The Book of Changes there are two hexagrams that contain references to what can be formed in the own city, and in what way it is formed. But before we turn to these two hexagrams, I would like to discuss one aspect of the system of this book that was often used in the classical Chinese J ching interpretation, and that may also help us come close to the meaning of these two hexagrams. This is the aspect of opposites that finds expression in the system of images and hexagrams of The Book of Changes.[28] The

25. Hex. 7, 6/3, ibid., p. 34.
26. Ibid., p. 622.
27. See p. 41.
28. In the Jao-te-ching, the affinity of opposites is a much-discussed princi-

attempt to grasp the meaning of a concept from its opposite, to enlighten both positions by the interplay of opposites, is not foreign to us, and we, too, have found that an affinity between opposites exists that does not express itself alone in contrast, but also in agreement.

The pairs of opposites that we have accepted in common usage were defined by the tradition of our thinkers, and probably also by the development of our language. A different way of looking at the world and another history of human traditions leads occasionally to other pairs of opposites. Aside from the opposites with which we, too, are familiar, we often find surprising ones. Especially from the interplay of pairs of opposites to which we are unaccustomed, we may often derive insight into the essence of a concept or a situation that is worthwhile to follow up.

Something else must be added. The system of The Book of Changes is the representation of a multidimensional world. Pairs of opposites should not be looked for only at the poles of a one-dimensional axis. Depending on the direction of view, there will be found a number of different opposites for every given concept or situation.

The system of line complexes lends itself particularly well to a discovery of such pairs of opposites. The mathematical precision of this system gives these established pairs of opposites a force that is almost compelling. The classical Chinese *J ching* interpretation has developed several methods for the establishment of such pairs. Three of them are often considered especially helpful to an understanding of the hexagrams. The first is the P'ang-t'ung; it consists of changing all six lines of a hexagram into their opposites. The second is the Ch'ien-kua, in which the whole hexagram is

---

ple; e.g., see Richard Wilhelm, *Laotse, Tao te King* (1957 ed.), p. 76 and passim. See also D. C. Lau, "The Treatment of Opposites in Laotse," *Bulletin of the School of Oriental and African Studies* 21 (1958):334–60.

turned on its head. And the third is the Chiao-kua, in which the two trigrams of a hexagram are interchanged.

Of these methods, the second appears to be the oldest. Its name means "hidden hexagrams," and it seems to be based on the insight that opposites lie hidden within one another. This method is already displayed in the sequence of the hexagrams in our text, in which such opposites as a rule follow one another. It is then developed further in the Miscellaneous Notes. The method of P'ang-t'ung, a word one is tempted to translate as *coincidentia oppositorum*, can be shown to have existed in Han times. It might, however, be older.

To demonstrate how these methods express themselves in the system of The Book of Changes, I have chosen Hexagram 49, 𝒦o, Revolution. An application of the three methods results in the following image with this hexagram:

Hexagram 49, Revolution

P'ang-t'ung	Ch'ien-kua	Chiao-kua
Hexagram 4,	Hexagram 50,	Hexagram 38,
Youthful Folly	The Caldron	Opposition

The effervescent dynamic of the forty-ninth hexagram, expressed by the image of fire in the lake, is one of the strongest in the whole Book of Changes.[29] The Judgment text contains the same words as The Creative: "Supreme success, furthering through perseverance." The text of the dominating line of the hexagram, the nine in the fifth place, reads "The great man changes like a

29. Wilhelm-Baynes, pp. 189–92.

tiger. Even before he questions the oracle he is believed." And in the T'uan Commentary it is said "The time of revolution is really great."[30] But even this revolutionary situation carries with it conservative elements. It is the dawning of a new age, but also the arrival of the stable order of a new age. And thus the Image text says: "The superior man sets the calendar in order and makes the time clear." In the regulated order of time, the calendar, the meaning of the new age, is laid down.

Hexagram 50, *Jing*, The Caldron, stands in the Ch'ien-kua relationship.[31] Here the conservative situation is stabilized in religious ritual. The Image text says here: "The superior man rectifies the [social] positions and thereby consolidates the [heavenly] mandate."[32]

The word *consolidate* in the original text means "to freeze." Fate is frozen here into a block of ice. And therefore the two dominating lines have conservative images: The caldron with gold or even jade rings, images in which the symbolism of the material strengthens the function of the implement in its irrefutable position. Even the envy of the companions evoked by such a position (nine in the second place) cannot alter it. The caldron contains nourishment, and the man of the caldron commands the economic situation.

And yet, even this situation, so opposite to the revolutionary, again contains dynamic elements. This is already expressed in the beginning line in which the stable institution of marriage is broken in order to remove the obstruction, then at the nine in the third and the nine in the fourth place, where partly meaningless and unfortunate changes occur, which finally undermine trust in the conservative situation. This is expressed most clearly in

30. Ibid., p. 636.
31. Ibid., pp. 193–97.
32. I depart here somewhat from my father's translation.

the Miscellaneous Notes, which reads: "The caldron means taking up the new."[33]

On the other hand Hexagram 49 stands against the fourth, Youthful Folly,[34] the seemingly aimless fermentation of the still unenlightened, in whom curiosity, sometimes irksome, alternates with hesitation in the face of danger. The revolutionary, with clear goals, is contrasted here to the dull fool who may yield to the brazen will of another to a degree that goes counter to his nature and fate. (The six in the third place clothes this in the image of a girl who, in the face of a man of bronze, loses possession of herself.) Here the revolutionary dynamic is not opposed to the conservative static, but the conscious pursuit of an aim is opposed to the aimless. However, the youthful fool carries the germ of the revolutionary within himself. He is in harmony with his time, he yields to it without reflection and absorbs its trends and conditions immediately. In the dominating line of this hexagram, the text shows an affinity with the direction of movement of Hexagram 49.

Finally, Hexagram 38, K'uei, Opposition, is placed against the forty-ninth. This hexagram is a reversal of the two trigrams. We have here, just as in Hexagram 49, the two irreconcilable sisters whose changed roles do not add to their harmony.[35]

In Hexagram 38 we find, in contrast to the forty-ninth, the man who is opposed to the revolutionary by temperament. The revolutionaries appear to him as dirt-encrusted pigs, a wagonful of devils. He already has his bow drawn against them. But in the last instance he lays his bow aside (upper nine).[36] For even he

33. Wilhelm-Baynes, p. 641.
34. Ibid., pp. 20–24.
35. Ibid., pp. 147–50.
36. The text of this line seems to have been changed considerably some time during the 7th century B.C.; see *Journal of the American Oriental Society* 79 (1959):279. The interpretation of its original meaning is thus in doubt. The

must realize that the conditions the revolutionary wants to remove, in which the wagon is drawn back, the oxen are halted, and people's hair and noses are cut off (six in the third place), cannot continue. So he stands isolated (nine in the fourth place and upper nine) between the camps. Should he continue to serve the old lord whom he meets in the dark street (nine in the second place)? Should he join his revolutionary companion who bites his way through the wrapings (six in the fifth place)? He chooses the second way. He realizes that the revolutionaries are not the robbers he presumed them to be; his doubts disappear and he joins their ranks. But even with the dangers to be overcome in this companionship, he retains his individuality (Image text).

All three of these opposites contribute to an understanding of the revolutionary situation, of the revolutionary aim, and of the revolutionary personality; partly by contrast, partly by affinity.

By setting up pairs of opposites according to these methods, one does not necessarily arrive at the number three. There are cases in which two opposites coincide. This is the case for example, with Hexagram 13, *T'ung Jên*, Fellowship with Men.[37] Here reversing the hexagram and exchanging the trigrams lead to the same result. It is curious that loneliness, standing aside, or eremitism are not among the opposites. Instead, following the P'ang-t'ung method, we arrive at Hexagram 7, *Shih*, The Army, and following the Ch'ien-kua and the Chiao-kua methods, Hexagram 14, *Ta Yu*, Possession in Great Measure.

Hexagram 13, Fellowship with Men

(probable) older text quoted in the *Tso-chuan* reads: "Isolated through opposition. The robber draws the bow against him. Alas, that the nephew follows the aunt. After six years he excapes." This reading is almost diametrically contrary to our present text.

37. Wilhelm-Baynes, pp. 56–59.

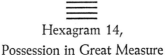

Hexagram 7,   Hexagram 14,
The Army   Possession in Great Measure

With the help of these two opposites, the character of Hexagram 13 becomes clear. In contrast to the seventh and the fourteenth hexagrams, it emerges that the thirteenth hexagram is not concerned with every possible type of human fellowship, but with the free association of free people outside the bondage of the traditional.

Without these pairs of opposites, the word of the Judgment, "Fellowship with men in the open" (literally, in the wilderness) could be overlooked too easily or misunderstood, especially since the later layers of the book obscure this circumstance somewhat. The later layers would prefer to see these people of wild determination, who congregate around the campfire under the clear sky, brought back to law and under proper leadership. But these men discuss conditions with like-minded comrades (Image),[38] and they think of the fellowship with men in the clan as a disgrace (six in the second place). Nothing results from their plans of action for a long time (nine in the third place and nine in the fourth place), and they finally return to the suburban meadow for the communal sacrifice without having achieved their aim (upper nine).

The seventh hexagram,[39] in contrast to the thirteenth, stands not for isolation, but for the unfree fellowship of the army, led by heroes (Judgment), decorated by the king, and used by him (nine in the second place and upper six). Discipline rules here (beginning six) even in retreat (six in the fourth place). The bonds of the enforced fellowship of the army may lead to a peculiar splintering. This is described in the six in the fifth place, as the

38. The Image text might be translated in this way.
39. Wilhelm-Baynes, pp. 31–35.

contrast between brothers of whom the older leads the army and the younger transports corpses. This is probably a reference to the splitting of personality under overpowering pressure from without. The carrying of corpses is one of the unfortunate but necessary functions of the army (six in the third place). But that this action can result in the splitting of the personality into unequal twins, shows to what extent the opposition to a free fellowship with men can develop.

Another opposite, surprisingly enough, is Hexagram 14, Possession in Great Measure.[40] Great possessions, even in a material sense, is seen as good fortune (Judgment) and a blessing of Heaven (upper nine) in the world image of The Book of Changes. Conceived and used in the right way, it provides access to possibilities not available without it (nine in the second place and nine in the third place), and in the best sense it forms a personality that, in its care for others, is accessible as well as dignified (six in the fifth place).

The inherent problem that may be encountered by one who possesses lies in possessing in the proper manner, and not being possessed by one's property (another reading of the nine in the fourth place would be: he does not rest on his affluence), and that one obeys Heaven's good will also, as a possessor, or especially as possessor (Image).

Now, why is this hexagram in particular opposed to the thirteenth hexagram, Fellowship with Men? Superficially speaking, one might say that it embodies the material aristocracy as opposed to the intellectual proletariat. It seems to me, however, that the contrast lies deeper. Possession in great measure may lead to beautiful and blessed achievements; with greater certainty, however, it will lead to the isolation of the person (beginning nine, especially Little Image, and nine in the fourth place).[41] This is a

40. Ibid., pp. 59–63.
41. Ibid., p. 458.

consequence of the situation as such, no personal blame is connected with it. When the fire no longer blazes under the sky, but burns in the sky above, intimacy within the fellowship of men becomes difficult if not impossible. Possession, material as well as intellectual, isolates; the battle for an idea brings people together.

We can see from these examples how the interplay of opposites is represented in The Book of Changes. Several of the resulting points of view may serve at the same time as background to a commentary on the formation within the own city.

There are two hexagrams in particular that deal with the situation of the own city at the time of formation. Both are very dynamic, even excited, images. The environment of the own city is, as we have seen, a design tending toward permanence, and the concept of formation has a permanent, even normative aspect. However, the establishment of this form is an exciting, even dangerous, moment necessitating weighty and quick decisions. If the casting is to be successful, quick and decisive action is necessary at the determining moment.

The first of these two hexagrams is Hexagram 43, *Kuai*, Breakthrough.[42]

Here the lower trigram and both nuclear trigrams are the creative. Above all these creative signs stands the lake, the dark massed clouds in the sky, or the irrigation canal built too high and therefore inclined to flooding. The break-through that is about to occur here is seen as a cloudburst or the bursting of a dam. The latently creative, in many ways part of this image, becomes the object of a sudden, and therefore dangerous, fructification. If in the decisive moment this conjunction is unsuccessful, the creative is drowned, and the formation cannot occur. In the Miscellaneous Notes, where

42. Ibid., pp. 166–70.

the order frequently deviates from the order of our text, this hexagram is the last and decisive one of the whole series. The Judgment to this hexagram reads:

> One must resolutely make the matter known at the court of the king. The call of the hatching bird [the truthful call] indicates danger. One must announce it to one's own city. Resorting to arms does not further. It furthers one to undertake something.[43]

The moment of formation is thus seen here as something that concerns everyone, and that must be brought to the attention of the king, the representative of Heaven among men, and the originator and manager of ordered and binding institutions, even if he does not want to know anything about it. The temptation to meet the indicated danger of the coming new formation with the force of arms and thereby to prevent it, must under all circumstances be withstood. Directed energy and an awareness of the sense of direction of the coming innovation is, however, necessary. But the decisive sentence is: "One must notify one's own city." Calling out to the own city, the summons to the inherent structure of the self, brings forth the break-through. It is the word that creates formation.

So we find here the creative word that penetrates the structure of the self, the own city, and there brings about formation. The opposite to the forty-third hexagram in the P'ang-t'ung relationship is Hexagram 23, Po, Splitting Apart,[44] the image of decay and putrefaction, a situation in which it is not even indicated to have an aim.

The inherent hidden opposite in the Ch'ien-kua relationship is Hexagram 44, Kou, Coming to Meet,[45] the image of the girl who

43. I depart somewhat from my father's translation.
44. Wilhelm-Baynes, pp. 93–96.
45. Ibid., pp. 170–73.

is too accommodating. The *J ching* advises not to marry such a girl because one could not live with her permanently. The situation is unique and unusual but also very powerful, in which "everything under Heaven prospers splendidly," one of which the Commentary to the Decision says: "Great, indeed, is the meaning of the time of Coming to Meet."[46] The Image text speaks here also of an outcry or invocation, but not, as in Hexagram 43, to the own city but to the four quarters of Heaven.

In the Chiao-kua relationship, in which the trigrams are exchanged, stands Hexagram 10, *Lü*, Treading,[47] the image of the grasping of meaning and the actualization of meaning. This hexagram progresses steadily and without lingering and reaches its summit in the image of moral law.

In this configuration of opposites, man is called upon to bring about the break-through. At the stage of self-realization that the world image of the Book of Changes represents, man is, next to the divinity and next to the natural development of inherent tendencies, the third of the agencies who participate in formation. This participation, which is the calling of man, is fate and creates fate. He has to bring about the break-through here, breaking out of the squalor of decay and of the rigidity of a moral law. He has to accomplish the break-through in sovereign impartiality, responsive to conditions that may confront him, even when these are unusual and unique. He has to bring it about by calling out to the own city, by the creative word that is directed to the depth of the

46. Ibid., p. 609.
47. Ibid., pp. 44–47. This hexagram has been discussed above, pp. 73–77, see especially note 70.

self. Only in this way can the fate he creates, his own fate, be built into the continuum of his self and his world. As the Image text expresses it: The fate "which he dispenses reaches down to the bottom and he refrains from resting on his virtue."

How this formation is carried out in detail is spelled out by the line texts. Resoluteness and energy that are required seem to be less of a problem than the necessary care and circumspection. In the first line already one becomes powerfully aware of the urge to create in the face of corruption. One is "mighty in the forward-striding toes." The realization that the tendencies toward corruption are predominant, that the ridgepole is about to break, may be a prod to precipitous action. But one can only strive toward a goal he is capable of achieving. Caution, even guardedness, is still necessary here.[48]

At this point the process begins. The first call sounds; it is a call of alarm that advises to take up arms against all dangers, especially against the dangers of the dark and the night. If one is armed in this manner, it is only necessary to wait for the right moment, one's "own day."[49] This condition of armed waiting is easily followed by a frivolous feeling of power. To be powerful in the cheekbones, nevertheless, brings misfortune.[50] The resolve, not alone for battle but for the act of formation, must double, even when it leads into loneliness and into the rain, even when one is bespattered and murmured against. Expressed here is the insight that the act of formation, even when faced with a threatening catastrophe, requires a time to mature. Here the kind of energy manifested in powerful cheekbones is not called for, but the energy to endure, which even upon apparent setbacks and misunderstandings remains steadfast to its aims.

Now we have arrived at the most difficult point of formation.

48. See Hex. 28, Judgment and 6/1, ibid., pp. 111–12.
49. See Hex. 49, 6/2, ibid., p. 190.
50. See Hex. 58, especially 6/3, ibid., p. 229.

Lonely and misunderstood, one treads along his way, till walking comes hard. It seems one must continue to endure in order not to become untrue to his aims. Still, one must wait, and wait in blood.[51] Here the J ching gives unbelievable advice: one should let oneself be led like a sheep. The J ching anticipates that hardly anyone would be inclined to take this advice. The necessary foresight that would supplement the necessary energy is all too difficult to maintain under the circumstances. The man who seems to be losing his creative power takes recourse in his stubbornness. But only by giving up conscious aims for a time can he climb out of the pit.

Finally the moment has come, the sheeplike nature dissipates,[52] and one is in a position of great power. Now one can utilize his resolve again, double resolve: to root out all obstructions and to bring about a new formation. In this way, one walks in the middle, one acts from the center and remains free of blame.

At this stage the upper six adds the warning against wanting to create the break-through without call. Like the arrogant dragon of the upper nine of the first hexagram, one is presumptuous here and undertakes formation only through the conscious ego. Such a formation cannot last, and in the final result leads to misfortune.

The outlined way is onerous and full of difficulties. It does not lead to heroic victories and dazzling successes. The fate of creating fate is imposed on man; he must take care himself that the break-through does not swamp him, that the outbreak from the old and rigid follows conscious constructive ways. This fate to create fate requires an attitude difficult to maintain, which at best keeps one from making mistakes. For here the own city may no longer be abandoned as in the aforementioned prehistoric era, if the creation is to endure.

What has happened here? What has been formed here and how? A consideration of the forty-third hexagram makes par-

51. See Hex. 5, 6/4, ibid., p. 26.
52. See Hex. 34, 6/5, ibid., p. 135.

ticularly clear how, when they are reduced to the world image of the Book of Changes, the general and the specific relate to each other in perception and action. To begin with, as with all questions put to the oracle, the time situation is determined in which the questioner and his group are situated. If this concrete moment in time is clear, it will be placed in the configuration of opposites, again as with all consultations of an oracle, which for this concrete moment in time delineates the field of action. Thereupon it is clarified in which segment of the world, and in affinity or contrast to which powers in the world, this specific moment in time can become productive and fruitful. The pronouncements of the texts then give guidance as to what degree and in which way human action will become responsible for the formation of this moment. Formation is not always or entirely dependent on human action. Formation can be brought about by the influence of the divine, or it can be the product of pure "natural" development, or it can be the result of an interplay of several powers of the great trinity.

In our case, in the moment of the break-through, energetic and directed human action is indicated in order to shape the new formation. Kind and degree of human influence are not the same in every case. That will have become obvious from some of our earlier examples. Hexagram 43 provides, as mentioned, one of the two cases in the Book of Changes in which human influence is placed in relationship to the own city. The primordial structure beyond the threshold, beyond the world of phenomena, the unapparent, or as yet unapparent, structure of the own city is called upon to produce the formation.

The remarkable tension between directed energy and listening to the echoed call into the depth of the own self gives our situation its exciting and unique quality. To allow oneself to be guided by divine will, or to yield to natural development, are attitudes that are not foreign to human nature. But which energetic man with conscious aims would want to be led like a sheep by the preformed image in the own self? The paradox that nothing less than directed ambition is dependent in this case on the impulses of the unconscious, impulses that are literally "called forth," becomes incontrovertibly clear in the fourth line of our hexagram. The self-renunciation demanded here of the conscious, whose calling it is to act with directed ambition, seems in itself so paradoxical that even the *I ching* gives up hope that such advice will be followed. But only in this way will the waiting in blood come to an end and only in this way does one get out of the pit.

I shall not try to resolve this paradox here. Yet I would like to point out one circumstance that makes it still more pointed. The Book of Changes is not solely, or even predominantly, a book for mystics.[53] Rather, it is a book that offers guidance on how to act, and to suffer, in our world of appearances. For those who act and suffer in this world, the representation is closer than the prototype, and the own city as a phenomenon of our world closer than the mandala. For him, potential formation becomes a shape in space, the image becomes mere space, the process becomes the stage. The problems of the dying city thus emerge here with great clarity. At the stage of human self-realization achieved by the early Chou, the own city could no longer be abandoned. What Neumann calls the tension between the ego and the self[54] had come into effect. Neither of these two poles, not the self, nor the ego, could any longer be abandoned. The Book of Changes has given some thought to this problem in Hexagram 20, *Kuan*, Contemplation.[55] There the contemplation of our world has been put into a relationship with the contemplation of the own self. I cannot comment here in further detail.

53. On the amazing image of the "own city" in Iranian mysticism see Henri Corbin in *Eranos Jahrbuch 1960* 29 (1961): 100–107. In his lecture, Corbin actually used the German phrase *die eigene Stadt*.

54. See Erich Neumann, "Die Psyche als Ort der Gestaltung," ibid., pp. 13–56.

55. Wilhelm-Baynes, pp. 48–52, 440–45.

Instead, we want to turn now to Hexagram 11, *T'ai*, Peace, in which the own city is also mentioned.[56]

If we bring this hexagram into the interplay of opposites, we arrive at the conclusion that within the described system all three possibilities coincide, that we are led on all three axes of opposites to the same hexagram, the twelfth, *P'i*, Stagnation. This conclusion has already been stated in Miscellaneous Notes where we find: "Stagnation and Peace stand in natural opposition to one another." This is one of the few cases of a unique contrast in the system of the Book of Changes. Only the last two hexagrams, After Completion and Before Completion, stand in a similar relationship.

The unambiguous opposition, not with war, but with stagnation, shows the special way the problem of peace is handled. Peace does not mean a condition here but a process, not a state of rest within oneself, but a development, and furthermore, not a formed structure, but a required formation.

This paradox is already hinted at in the order of the trigrams: heaven over earth, which would appear natural to us, is not the sign of peace, but earth over heaven, yin over yang. Heaven over earth is the sign of stagnation. This paradox has caused later commentators many headaches. Already in the later layers of the book a tendency can be discerned toward taking the outer appearance of peace for its essence and placing more emphasis on the tranquillity and harmony peace brings, than on the responsibility of establishing peace.

This tendency is not in itself unjustified. When the later layers see peace as a great comforter, when they see in peace the condition in which all injustice is expiated, when they see in it a mutual permeation, an all-embracing coherence, they come close to the

56. Ibid., p. 52.

meaning of the Chinese word employed here, *t'ai*, as well as to the tendencies of movement of the applicable trigrams. But for us the manifestation of peace, however correctly viewed, should not obscure its essence. Only in few other places it becomes so clear that for our book the world is a world of change in which not even the most beautiful manifestation can endure of itself and by itself. In addition, this hexagram contains one of the texts in which it is noted in what way and in what relationship to the own city this manifestation can be formed.

This text is allotted to the upper six of our hexagram. We must consider the hexagram as a whole, however, if we want to understand how the situation described in the upper six arose. In this hexagram, everything is movement toward the great, the all-encompassing, toward a condition in which low and high are equalized, in which everyone is accorded rights in consideration of his individuality, in which those distant are not neglected and those close by are not privileged, in which even the unsteady and roaming are gently enclosed in the complete image.

The texts of the hexagrams Peace and Stagnation repeatedly employ the same images and words. However, the conclusions drawn are contrary. In one, undertakings and decisive, directed action are indicated; in the other the stress falls on continuance. Already in the third line appears the warning: "no plane not followed by a slope." The condition of outer equilibrium, once achieved, cannot last. One may still enjoy the achieved condition, if he remains conscious of the law of life that there is no going not followed by a return: "Do not complain about this truth, enjoy the good fortune you still possess," says the text. The truth must, however, be faced; the warning not to yield to comfortableness is enclosed in it.[57]

At this stage and the next, peace makes its mightiest appearance. A condition in which one wishes to remain is achieved. The dy-

57. See Hex. 19, 6/3, ibid., p. 50.

namic tendencies of the beginning period are still in effect, the equilibrium has not yet separated into its parts. Wealth is still shared, equality is still upheld. More and more, however, manifestations become appearances, and the maintenance of equality becomes condescension. So the next line, the ruler of the hexagram, commands a self-renunciation of a drastic kind, which is seen in the image of the prince who gives his daughter in marriage to a barbarian lord. By means of this great personal sacrifice not only peace is maintained, but new worlds are opened up. This situation is the richest in blessings and good fortune in the hexagram.

At the top line the appearance is then destroyed. The text states: "The wall falls back into the moat. Use no army now. Announce this fate to your own city. Perseverance brings humiliation."[58]

Here the appearance of the city is brought into relationship with the primordial image of the own city. The enclosing circle of the primordial image has become a protecting rampart, a line of defense, behind which it seemed possible to settle down in peace. A line of defense, however, does not guarantee peace; as a manifestation it is subject to the law of decay. No exertion of military might can hold back this decay. An attempt to maintain the existing condition can bring only humiliation.

In this exciting moment of highest danger the book advises again to call out to the own city. The wording here is almost, but not quite, the same as in the forty-third hexagram. There it was simply a "call," the "calling forth" of the primordial image. Here the call has content: To the own city fate has to be called out. What has here been translated as "fate," is actually a divine command, or the mandate of Heaven. Still more distinctly than in the forty-third hexagram, man here becomes the executor of divine commands, the handy man of God. He executes these demands by a renewed turning toward the primordial image within his own self; he executes these through himself. No created form gives security any-

58. I differ here somewhat from my father's translation.

more to his existence. Not only his own person, but the peace of the world is about to decay. There is no longer a place where one can protect or hide oneself; there are no longer any opportunities to avoid one's own responsibility. One is placed at the seat of the shaper of fate, a fate moreover, that concerns not only his own person but the peace of his world.

Formation here, too, is carried out by the word, by the call, here by the call that carries fate. If this call succeeds, we are led to the beautiful text of the upper nine of the twenty-sixth hexagram: "One attains the way of heaven."[59] What is here translated as "way," is not the Tao; the word employed here means a small path, a narrow lane. By the proclamation of divine commands in the own self, one therefore attains here: *For peace, a path.*

59. Wilhelm-Baynes, p. 106.

V

THE INTERACTION OF
HEAVEN, EARTH, AND MAN

I

Around the turn of our era, there lived a man in China who is as well known for the poetic products of his youth as for the philosophical treatises of his old age. This was Yang Hsiung,[1] who, by virtue of his poetic talent, attracted the court's attention soon after his arrival in the capital. This period in China's history was one in which the art of the word was highly reputed. The so-called *fu*, the artistic form in vogue at that time, combined, in a remarkably austere style, a mastery of the literary tradition with a sumptuously hued and richly metaphorical expression. Rhythm, rhyme, and compositional structure also dominated longer poetic works, in a dimension that often rendered to them an enchanting beauty. Nevertheless, this poetic form was not placed exclusively nor perhaps even primarily at the disposal of poetic creation. Its position was also due to the circumstance that political allusions and political admonitions concealed in poetic dress could be submitted to the rulers, whose authoritarian position enabled them to resist being

1. 53 B.C.–A.D. 18. See David Richard Knechtges, *The Han Rhapsody: A Study of the Fu of Yang Hsiung (53 B.C.–A.D. 18)* (New York and London: Cambridge University Press, 1976).

accosted in a more direct way. Clothed in the alluring beauty of poetic form, the *fu* served also to open the ear of the emperors to desires that transcended the function of the strictly poetic.[2]

Yang Hsiung was a master of this style. We are indebted to him, among other things, for the poetic description of his provincial capital in western China,[3] for the depiction of an imperial palace,[4] and for the almost breath-taking portrayal of an imperial hunt.[5] We are further obliged to him for an ode to wine, and finally, for an ode to poverty.[6] This ode makes Yang Hsiung's ambiguity particularly evident. Constructed as a dialogue with an allegorical figure of Poverty, the ode describes here the poverty of his youth and the indigence of his years of manhood, when due to his poverty it seems that friendship and sociability remained denied to him. He continues to describe how he fled from Poverty, how it pursued him everywhere, and his final attempts to banish it with vehement words. In reply, and not without resentment, Poverty explains to him how without her, political and social conditions fall into a state of corruption, and what the formation of personality owes her:

> Did I not teach you
> By gradual usage, indifferent to endure
> Summer's heat and winter's cold?
> And that which neither heat nor cold can touch—
> Is it not eternal as the Gods?
> I, Poverty,

2. See Hellmut Wilhelm, "The Scholar's Frustration," in *Chinese Thought and Institutions*, ed. John K. Fairbank (Chicago: University of Chicago Press, 1957), pp. 310–19, 398–403; and, extensively, Knechtges, *Han Rhapsody*.

3. All the pieces mentioned are translated and/or discussed in Knechtges.

4. Also translated by E. von Zach in *Sinica* (1927), pp. 190–93, and in *Die chinesische Anthologie*, ed. Ilse Fang (Cambridge, Mass.: Harvard University Press, 1958), pp. 93–98.

5. Also translated in Zach, *Anthologie*, pp. 117–25.

6. Arthur Waley, *The Temple and Other Poems* (London: G. Allen & Unwin, 1923), pp. 76–80.

Turned from you the envy of the covetous, taught you to fear
Neither Chieh the Tyrant nor the Robber Chih.
Others, my master,
Quake behind bolt and bar, while you alone
Live open to the world.
Others by care
And pitiful apprehension are cast down,
While you are gay and free.

And Poverty, full of resentment, snatches up her garment, and rises, in order to abandon Yang Hsiung forever. In the meantime, Yang has perceived the folly of his lament; he appeals to Poverty and asks her for forgiveness.

Then Poverty came back and dwelt with me,
Nor since has left my side.[7]

In his later years Yang Hsiung began to doubt the value of poetry. He then wrote a book of discourses, which imitates Confucius' Analects, and bears the title: *Words of Stringent Admonition*.[8] In this book Yang attempts to apply the classical tradition, and specifically the Confucian tradition, to his own time situation. In the preservation of social institutions and customs, and in the maintenance of ethical rules of conduct attributed to Confucius, the book is remarkably stern, even rigid. Yang emerges as a representative of traditional orthodoxy, and he breaks with his own earlier tendencies of seeing man's relation to his own times and environment in poetic images. In reply to a direct question, he disavows his own poetic products with the words: "A grown man no

7. The ode calls to mind the "Lady Poverty" of St. Francis. Both Yang and the Saint had the daring to garb their acceptance of poverty in the image of a courtship. With this, however, the similarity stops.

8. Translation by E. von Zach, *Yang Hsiung's Fa-yen (Worte Strenger Ermahnung)* (Batavia, 1939). I have retained Zach's translation of the title, even though it is, of course, not literal. It characterizes well, however, the spirit of the little book.

longer occupies himself with such trifles."[9] And in a different passage, he equates his poetical works with blossoms and his philosophy with the fruits, and says: "I despise those who only pick my blossoms, but have no desire to eat my fruits."[10]

Yang Hsiung's turning away from the artistic and the creative, and his turning toward established institutions and old traditions, may at first glance be astonishing, especially since Yang was completely in possession of poetic talents. He could, however, deduce his position from Confucius, who, with perhaps too much modesty, once called himself a transmitter and not an innovator.[11] Confucius also attributed a leading role to traditional institutions. However, upon closer observation, the difference between Yang and Confucius becomes evident. The preservation and strengthening of a tradition was justified for Confucius, inasmuch as it signified the representation of a primordial relationship or of an archetypal situation. Moreover, he lived during a chaotic time, a period that longed for stable guiding principles and exemplary rules of conduct. For Yang Hsiung, however, the justification for an attitude or action depended on the tradition in itself. Tradition was, for him, the work of man, and above all, the work of Confucius, or rather of a somewhat idealized and mythologized Confucius, who was not always in complete agreement with the historical figure. If something could be traced back to Confucius or to this image of Confucius, then it required no further justification. Moreover, Yang lived in an era during which temporal institutions had attained a nature of inviolability, even though they had been established by present rulers, and not by the sages of antiquity; and even though they brought personal ambition and hunger for power to the forefront, and not valid archetypes. The compelling nature

9. Ibid., pp. 6–7.
10. Ibid., p. 24.
11. See p. 70.

of such institutions, decorated, as they usually were, with traditional embellishments, was something that not even the philosopher was able to evade. It was inherent in the premises of his system. And Yang Hsiung's position during his era and his reputation in posterity were influenced by his attitude toward this problem.[12] Yang Hsiung yielded almost without reservation to the leadership of these institutions. His contribution to the topic of this year's meeting originates in his tragic realism. During a period that has the tendency to concede an hypertrophied position to human institutions, Yang Hsiung contributes something curiously modern and timely.

Yang Hsiung's answer to the question of by what means and in which direction man should allow himself to be led, both in conduct and action, can be traced back to his view of the problem of chaos and order. For him, the restoration and maintenance of order was man's most urgent task, as it was for every Confucian of the imperial era. This consummate man, in his words: the sage, and among his endowments, the human spirit, were the instruments with which to create such an order. He was once asked why there could be no return to the state of high antiquity, when men lived in peace without any legal and moral orders; he answered with keen trenchancy: "Those times of high antiquity are despised by the sage . . . [Legal and moral orders are necessary], the sage does not want to know anything about those times of high antiquity."[13] The passion of this answer demonstrates how essential this subject seemed to Yang. He does not want to know anything about an innate system of relations, which has not been consciously created by the human spirit, even if such a system meets the needs of a community perfectly. With equal passion he condemns Lao-tse,

12. See Fritz Jäger, "Yang Hsiung und Wang Mang, "Sinica-Sonderausgabe 1 (1937):14–34.
13. Zach, p. 17.

who attributes the meaning of the world and of life to the epiphanies from darkness and chaos. He contrasts order with chaos, and clarity with darkness. His order is created by man, and it expresses itself in worldly traditions and institutions. And his clarity is the clarity of the human spirit.

This titanically exacting attempt to sever man from his origins in chaos and darkness, in other words, to uproot man, is common to many Confucian philosophers of the Imperial Age. Yang Hsiung is the earliest and probably the most unequivocal and most impassioned representative of this movement. In his life, Yang became hopelessly entangled in the gray-knitted mesh of human orders.[14] In his teachings he attempts to become master of them.

These teachings will not be pursued here in detail. However, several items from these teachings may aid in illustrating Yang's solution to the problem posed. Yang views man as a member of the great trinity: heaven, earth, and man, wherein Confucian philosophy had placed him, by virtue of the development of the insights gathered from the Book of Changes.[15] He also recognizes heaven as life-giving and earth as the provider of form.[16] Nevertheless, man is for Yang the crucial point. He once said: "Someone who understands the nature of heaven, earth, and man is a universal man of learning; someone who understands the nature of heaven and earth, but not of man, is an artisan."[17]

It is thus bestowed upon man to understand heaven and earth. This understanding is no longer solely the concern of religion, but is a matter for scholarly calling. Heaven's effect is limited for him: "As for my view about heaven, I see only its unconscious, unin-

14. See Goethe's "Mich ängstigt das Verfängliche . . . , Das grau-gestrickte Netz."
15. See, for instance, Zach, p. 36.
16. Ibid., p. 68.
17. Ibid., p. 66.

[131]

tentional creating. . . . How is it to have the power to render form?"[18]

And it is dependent on man: "Man cannot achieve success without heaven's aid, heaven cannot dispense happiness and affliction without suitable people."[19]

Among men, it is the sage, and among the sage's gifts, the human spirit, that Yang brings into prominence. In an almost dithyrambic chapter he replied to questions about the human spirit, a chapter in which his diction occasionally even suggests that of the Taoists:

> How wonderful after all is the human spirit! If we hold it fast, it remains with us; if we neglect it, we lose it. It is only the sage who always retains the spirit and never releases it. The sage uses his spirit for the exploration of this world's innermost secrets, to bring about order and peace in the world, to be of use to the living beings and to shape harmoniously the relations between heaven and man, so that a dissociating partition is not established between them.[20]

It is thus the human spirit that establishes the harmony of the world, and it even forces heaven into the constraint of human order. "Creator Spiritus!" Nevertheless, what is creating is the *human* spirit, and the creation is a *worldly* order.

According to the foregoing, Yang Hsiung appears as the great rationalist of his age. He appears, moreover, so much preoccupied with the traditions and institutions of his period, that his contributions might be considered as of little more than historical interest.[21]

18. Ibid., p. 16. Erich Neumann calls the phenomenon "the shrinkage of heaven" (*Krise und Erneuerung* [Zurich, 1961], p. 28).

19. Zach, p. 50.

20. Ibid., p. 21.

21. This preoccupation was so intense that Yang developed a nationalism that is alien to early Confucianism. The order of China is for him the standard order. When he was asked what he understood by "China," he answered: "The land where government rests on the doctrine of the five relationships . . , the land which lies in the center of the world, this land is China. Are there really any human beings outside of this land?" (Zach, p. 17).

If we possessed nothing more of his beyond the *Fa-yen*, then not very much could be added to what has already been said. However, Yang was not only the ideological strategist, he was also philosopher and poet.[22] And he clothed his teaching of human orders in a well-planned systematic work, in which he projects the system and the insights of the Book of Changes onto his era.

This is the *T'ai-hsüan Ching*, the Book of the Great Mystery. The word *hsüan*, translated here as "mystery,"[23] is extremely complex; it was used a great deal by the Confucians, as well as by the Taoists of Yang's and of the following period. What he himself understood by it, he once expressed by the following words:

> The Mystery, in its secret way, extends to the myriad species, yet does not display its shape. Taken and molded from emptiness and nothingness, it engenders the circle. It associates with the divine luminaries and determines patterns. It penetrates and unites with antiquity and the present in order to develop the various species. It extends and arranges the *yin* and *yang* and produces breath.[24]

And in another place he says: "The Mystery determines heaven's way, earth's course, and the way of man."[25]

The mystery is thus something that is by itself (*tzu-jan*),[26] and something that cannot be further reduced.

The Book of the Great Mystery is an imitation of the Book of Changes, which Yang Hsiung held in great esteem. He quoted it

22. Besides being a poet, Yang also dealt in detail with the language of his time, more particularly with dialectology. Paul Serruys has treated these interests of Yang extensively. Also in this regard, Yang appears amazingly "modern."

23. Zach translates this title *The Book of the Great Silence*. This translation is rather romantic but not quite accurate. In the *I ching*, *hsüan* is the color of heaven and the color of the blood of the male dragon.

24. Translated by David R. Knechtges, "Yang Shyong, the *Fuh*, and Hann Rhetoric" (Ph.D. diss., University of Washington, 1968).

25. See Fung Yu-lan, *A History of Chinese Philosophy*, trans. Derk Bodde (Princeton, N.J.: Princeton University Press, 1953), pp. 139–40.

26. Ibid.

often, and in an ode to the Great Mystery[27] he stated what he owed to this book, and even his indebtedness to Lao-tse. However, in the *I ching* he essentially saw a book about the way of heaven.[28] Man's role in this book's system would not and could not satisfy him, since the rigidity of the orders in his time and in his system was at too great a variance with the vast freedom of the *I ching*.[29] For this reason he hardened the free and infinite possibility of change into a cyclical movement, within which genesis and passing are subject to inescapable laws. And for the image of change in his system he substituted the "idea in itself," the Great Mystery.

As a traditionalist and defender of the classics, Yang Hsiung was, of course, compelled to justify his attempt to transform the system of the *I ching*. He was not deterred from making such a justification, and more than once he stated that each time and each situation requires within itself a new presentation of the principles that are immutable: "Whenever clothes are new, they can be put on; whenever they are old, they have to be thrown away or mended."[30]

And in the *Fa-yen* he wrote the following dialogue:

Somebody asked: "Confucius was a transmitter and not a composer.[31] How could you dare to compose the *T'ai-hsüan ching*?" Yang answered: "The events of the past will have to be transmitted, writings can only be composed. T'ung-wu was my son whom I have raised, who, however, did not get old. Already at the age of nine he discussed with me this book on the mystery." The other one asked: "With what purpose did you

27. Partially translated in ibid., p. 138.

28. Zach, p. 31.

29. It might be mentioned in passing that the institutionalization of the insights of the Book of Changes started earlier than Yang Hsiung. The later layers of the book already deal with such ideas. See Liu Pai-min, "The First Principle of Eventology of the I ching" (Chinese), *The New Asia Journal* 4, no. 2 (Feb. 1960) :1–64.

30. See Zach, p. 19. See also his stand against overblown institutional conservatism, p. 43.

31. *Lun-yü*. 7.1; James Legge, *The Chinese Classics* (London, 1865), 1:195.

write the *T'ai hsüan ching?*" Yang answered: "In the interest of humaneness and justice." The other one asked: "Which writer would not write in the interest of humaneness and justice?" Yang answered: "Certainly, but only the orthodox writer."[32]

Yang's book is based on a system of line complexes, just as the Book of Changes. The hexagrams are replaced by tetragrams, four-lined symbols, in which the single line can not only be undivided and divided, but also twice divided, so that he arrives at a sum total of three to the fourth power or eighty-one tetragrams. He rigorously coordinated the position of the single lines with administrative and social institutions. Just like the hexagrams in the Book of Changes, the tetragrams have a name and commentary that correspond to the Judgment. Thereupon follow nine texts, in a way corresponding to the line texts in the Book of Changes. They are not, however, associated with the lines of the tetragrams, but describe the steps of ascent and decline of the situation marked in the tetragram. The first four characterize a success progressing in stages; the fifth usually describes the zenith, and the sixth through ninth describe the steps of decreasing effect, and the ultimate return to the point of departure. Commentatory explanations, which correspond to the Little Images, are attached to these nine texts. In each case he specified which of the hexagrams in the Book of Changes the tetragram imitates.

Yang Hsiung characterized the nine steps in the following manner:

> Therefore the appearance of thoughts in the mind represents the first [stage]; the turning over [of these thoughts] represents the second; their formulation into definite ideas, the third; the extension of these [into action], the fourth; their manifestation [in resulting achievements], the fifth; the attainment of greatest [achievement], the sixth; [subsequent] decline and loss, the seventh; disintegration and collapse,

32. Zach, p. 24. Yang has been attacked frequently on account of his *T'ai-hsüan ching* and has written several rebuttals. One of these has been translated by Zach, *Die chinesische Anthologie*, pp. 834–40.

the eighth; destruction and annihilation, the ninth. The first [of these stages] is that of the birth of consciousness, than which there is nothing prior. The fifth is that of central harmony, than which there is nothing more perfect. The ninth is the seat of suffering, than which there is nothing more tormenting.[33]

It is interesting that in this sequence the zenith of manifestation follows one step after the culminating point of inherent development.

As an example, I would like to examine the first tetragram of the *T'ai-hsüan ching*, which at the same time is the foundation of Yang Hsiung's system. The tetragram consists of four undivided lines; its name is *Chung*, The Center. The tetragram reads: "The power of the Yang, still submerged, is budding in the Yellow Palace. Its reliability is nowhere outside of the center."

Yellow, originally the color of the earth in the Book of Changes, gradually evolves into the color of the center in that book also.[34] The Yellow Palace is an image often used in later mystical speculation and in alchemy.[35] The center, and only the center, is the place where the male yang force develops in the absolute, the place from which it begins its imperturbable and inevitable (dependable) path to leadership.

The nine steps of the text read:

1. "Chaotic and boundless, in darkness."

33. Fung-Bodde translation.

34. E.g., see the Little Image commentaries to Hex. 30, 6/2, Wilhelm-Baynes, p. 537; 40, 9/2, ibid., p. 592; 50, 6/5, ibid., p. 645.

35. Later Taoists locate the Yellow Palace in the upper part of the head, as against the Cinnabar Field, which is in the lower part of the body. These two centers were, even though by different names, already mentioned in the 6th century B.C. See Hellmut Wilhelm, "Eine Chou-Inschrift über Atemtechnik," *Monumenta Serica* 13 (1948):385–88. David Knechtges, on the other hand, suggests with good evidence that the term *huang-kung* (yellow palace) refers here to the tonic of the pentatonic scale.

Added commentary: "Chaotic and boundless: concentrate on this with perseverance."[36]

At this step, the centering function of the center has not yet appeared. It reminds one of the Tohuwabohu of our myth of creation. The T'uan Commentary of Hexagram 3 in the Book of Changes, *Chun*, Difficulty at the Beginning, contains a similar image: "... chaos and darkness prevail while Heaven is creating."[37]

For Yang and his system this means an infernal step that is loathed by the sage as much as disorderly prehistory, something he nevertheless also had to postulate in the beginning. It is this nothingness that precedes consciousness.

2. "The spirit battles with the Mystery. The battle lines are drawn by Yin and Yang."

Added commentary: "The spirit battles with the Mystery: Good and evil are undifferentiated."

Here we are once again reminded of our myth of creation. It is a matter of the knowledge of good and evil. This knowledge is achieved in conflict, and here the spirit appears for the first time as a combatant. It struggles with the mystery as did Jacob with the angel. Knowledge of good and evil, the foundation of every moral order, must be forced from the Mystery by means of conflict. Yin and yang, the male and the female principles, determine the conflict's conditions. Good and evil do not appear in the early layers of the Book of Changes; the Wings occasionally make use of them, however.

3. "The dragon comes forth from the center. Stretching head and tail. He can be taken as a constant measure."

---

36. This is the term *chen*, consistently translated as "perseverance" in Wilhelm-Baynes. It is, of course, far from certain that Yang Hsiung used it in this sense. One commentary suggests the meaning "correct," i.e., unsullied by human desires.

37. Wilhelm-Baynes, p. 399.

Added commentary: "The dragon comes forth from the center: his creative force becomes apparent."

The dragon is known to us from the first hexagram as the symbol of the creative principle. However, the laborious path of the Creative in the dragon ballad of this hexagram has been omitted here. It needs only to stretch itself. It acts from the center, and through its appearance alone it already fulfills its function of bringing the circumference[38] to a dependable form that can serve as a constant measure. The image of the dragon awaking from sleep and stretching itself, who by his existence alone creates a field of ordered tension, is not without charm.

4. "Lowly and void, without causation. Receiving in great measure of nature and destiny is at a standstill."

Added commentary: "The obstruction of the lowly and void: he cannot receive in great measure."

The field of ordered tension is created; it is nevertheless still without content and without gradations, and thus nothing can happen at this point. Such a void state of equilibrium opposes human action. The development of human nature and the evolving of human destiny in historical dimension requires yet another potential, which is described in the next line.

5. "The sun in the zenith of heaven. It is furthering to use the moment in time to become master."

Added commentary: "The sun in the zenith of heaven: the elevated has his appropriate position."

The noon sun symbolizes literally the tetragram's zenith; the center has been raised into the center of heaven. The ruler assumes his position. He owes it alone to the favor of circumstance and his own resolve. With this, a hierarchical element is added to the flat field of ordered tension.

---

38. Circumference is the name of the second tetragram of the *T'ai-hsüan ching*.

6. "The fullness of the moon wanes. It would be better to create light in the West."

Added commentary: "The fullness of the moon wanes: the light begins to retreat."

With this we now enter into the descending section of the curve. The possibility is still given to create light in the west, that is in the direction of the final decline.

7. "Cleared wine. Fire harbors nourishment, water contains perseverance."

Added commentary: "What cleared wine contains: this is the measure of investing officials."

The word translated here as "cleared wine" denotes wine's condition directly after the termination of the fermentation process. It symbolizes the position of the civil servants. With this it is indirectly intimated what must happen to the man who becomes a civil servant, and who thus enters into the ranks of the social elite, as seen from Yang Hsiung's time situation. The turbulence and opaqueness of the fermentation must lie completed behind him. Then his position contains sustenance—here in the sense of the twenty-seventh hexagram of the Book of Changes—and he then has the necessary perseverance. The firewater is semantically decomposed into its parts here. Whether or not such a process can be conducted with actual wine remains of course an open question.

8. "Yellow is not yellow. The constancy of autumn is overturned."

Added commentary: "Yellow is not yellow: central power is lost."

Here we are approaching the end. The center's color is contested. (This formulation recalls dogmas of the Sophist schools, something Yang Hsiung attacked especially vehemently.) Due to this the center loses its power. And even autumn's beauty is deprived of its wonder.

9. "The life-giving spirit topples. Power and form return home."

Added commentary: "The returning home of the life-giving spirit: time cannot be overcome."

The end is irrevocable, determined only by the course of time. The concept of order induces by necessity the end. And thus we fall again into chaos and darkness. The inexorableness of this development may shock us. Nevertheless, the tragic realist Yang Hsiung remains true to his system. The system requires the fall of the life-giving spirit. And thus he looks calmly into the eye of the return of chaos and darkness.

Yang Hsiung's first tetragram, *Chung*, The Center, is based on Hexagram 61 of the Book of Changes, *Chung-fu*, Inner Truth. The line complexes of these two signs clearly demonstrate the difference between the two texts:

Yang Hsiung's symbol for the Center consists of a fixed system of firm undivided lines. The Inner Truth, however, grows out of the center's softness under the protection of a strong exterior. The constituting lines of Inner Truth are yin lines. If one extirpates these lines of Inner Truth, then Yang's Center remains.

It can be demonstrated that Yang's concept of the Center gradually evolved from the Book of Changes. This is already evident from the numerical value he attaches to the symbols. For him it is also the Five, indeed the doubled Five.[39] This coordination is found in apocryphal speculations on the Book of Changes.[40] The Five is already found in the Great Treatise. Originally a celestial number, it is here a number of earth as well as of heaven.[41]

39. Fung-Bodde, p. 146.

40. See Schuyler Cammann, "The Magic Square of Three in Old Chinese Philosophy and Religion," *History of Religion* 1 (1961):37–80. Cammann deals here with the *Writing From the River Lo* and shows how this schema advances the concept of centrality.

41. See Wilhelm-Baynes, p. 310.

A comparison of the texts of the two signs makes it clear how incisive the development from one to the other has been. The sign Inner Truth is also the sign of dependability.[42] This dependability extends even to pigs and fishes, the most nonspiritual of animals. It does not originate in the knowledge of good and evil, but in open candor, ready for devotion, of the two middle lines, which constitute truth. The T'uan Commentary already wants to dislodge them from the Center, and wants to reserve this place for the yang lines nine in the second place and nine in the fifth place. The image of the central emptiness, which Yang Hsiung despises so much, the notion of unprejudiced candor, cannot be destroyed, however. The emptiness lends the sign essence, and its essence determines the adjacent nines. The text of nine in the second place reads: "A crane calling in the shade. Its young answers it. I have a good goblet. I will share it with you."[43]

It is not the spirit's power that constitutes the essence of these lines, but rather poetically expressed personal inclinations and common joys. And nine in the fifth place reads: "He possesses truth, which links as if by chains."

This text is probably taken from an old folk song. It contains an important hint for the problem of leadership. It is truth, not the spirit and not the power, that ties the ones led to the leader.

Both nines, which are further removed from the yin lines, show impulses of the spirit in a more uninfluenced form: the ulterior motives in nine at the beginning and the unsuccessful ambition in nine at the top.

If we now contrast this with Yang Hsiung's image of the Center, it seems to be characterized by the omission of the two central yin lines. An essential part of the content is taken away from it. Instead, he has diverted the Center from a Within to an Above. The Center no longer operates on the basis of inner truth, it rules powerfully

42. Ibid., p. 699.
43. Cf. ibid., pp. 237, 239, for these two quotes.

from above. This hierarchical elevation of the Center is again a position that has developed gradually. In the early Han era, the center was already equated with the position of the emperor, that is with the locus of worldly power.[44] Yang Hsiung sublimated the actuality of a political institution to the central principle of his philosophical system. He was able to do this only by making the Within into an Above.

In a time like ours, during which life is once again in danger of becoming lost in the maze of rational orders and worldly institutions, Yang Hsiung deserves renewed attention. We should not think little of him because he inserted the compelling nature of these orders and institutions into the premises of his system. He had to accept the manifestation of life as it offered itself to him, since "service" stood in the foreground of the offered, for him as for every Confucian. He could only serve within the framework of the given, and under the realities with which he had to come to terms—since in his time, as in ours, orders and institutions ruled and dominated powerfully.

The solutions he proposes are not, however, the solutions of an organizer or a lawgiver. As poet and linguist, Yang Hsiung could obtain information for his solutions from sources denied to the keepers of order. For him the word was still alive and not a dead instrument, and the image, even when he transformed it poetically, remained close to what was originally mythological. Yang Hsiung was indeed a realist. He was, however, a creative realist, and he allowed himself to be guided by the word and by the archetype, as much as by political, social, and psychological realities. And since the situation of our times corresponds to his in a certain way,

44. Again see Cammann, who also points out how it was attempted to add a numinous basis to this rationalized scheme. The cult of the deity T'ai-i, the Great Unique One, was built into the governmental ceremonies and into the centralized scheme. This attempt has not lasted for long.

it may be worthwhile to examine somewhat closer the solutions to the problem of leadership he proposed. In particular, I would like to devote a little time to two of his tetragrams, the twelfth, *T'ung*, The Boy, and the nineteenth, *Ts'ung*, The Following.

Yang Hsiung developed his twelfth tetragram from the fourth hexagram of the Book of Changes, *Meng*, Youthful Folly. Here the text of the tetragram reads: "The power of the Yang starts to be perceived. The things are childlike, they are still unconscious."

It is the yang potential alone that Yang Hsiung sees in this text. It is the veiled yang, which has not yet advanced towards consciousness. The text of the first of the nine steps reads:

1. "A simple child that does not awake. Meeting me [the ego] he abides in folly and confusion."

Added commentary: "A child that does not wake up: I am afraid he will end in obscurity."

As a beginning step, a point in time in the child's life is chosen here, in which the self confronts the ego for the first time. The ego is extrapolated here, and it turns into the symbol of the leader. Yang Hsiung the linguist may have been familiar with the Chinese word for "ego" used here, which signifies the suffering or enduring ego. The situation's pretension to awaken to an ego consciousness would include the insight that the ego is a life of suffering and enduring. The boy refuses to wake up; he remains preoccupied in a condition Yang Hsiung can only designate as folly and confusion. The light of the spirit remains closed to him.

2. "He manipulates the divining milfoil and heats the oracle tortoise. He emerges from the mud and enters the world of luster."

Added commentary: "To manipulate the milfoil and to heat the tortoise: this is the illustrious way [Tao]."

At this step the boy accepts leadership. It is, however, the leadership of irrational powers, which manifest themselves in divination. The self-limitation that lies in this attitude leads him out of the primitive mud into the world, which appears lustrous to him. In this way, the encounter of the self with the environment is accomplished successfully.

3. "The moment in time when the East lights up. He is, however, incapable of acting accordingly."

Added commentary: "The moment in time when the East lights up; why does he not follow this path?"

The light of the spirit dawns here. The boy is nevertheless too much a boy to let himself be led by the spirit. For this reason the despairing question of the commentary.

4. "With hesitation he follows the master who walks in front. The illustriousness of earlier bestowals."

Added commentary: "With hesitation he follows the master who walks in front: the illustriousness of the past is great."

Having found it impossible to follow the light of his own spirit, the boy is here inducted into the tradition by the teacher. He follows reluctantly. However, the attraction of what has been practiced for generations is strong enough to compel him to accept. It is the light of the past, a reflected light, offered to him indirectly through the mouth of the teacher, by which he now lets himself be led. This last aspect may have evoked his inhibitions. The word, which has been translated here as "bestowals," comprises the idea that the offerings of tradition are based on dispensations from above, indeed, divine dispensations. In this way he conquers his inhibitions and follows.

5. "The youthful fool gathering firewood in search of a rhinoceros. What he obtains is not pretty."

Added commentary: "The youthful fool gathering firewood in search of a rhinoceros: he obtains the uncommendable."

Yang Hsiung does not use the word *boy* here, but the word *youthful fool*, which he took from the Book of Changes. A boy who is mature enough to gather kindling wood, and therefore to perform useful work in an adult sense, attains, according to a passage in the

Book of Rites, a rise in status due to this work, which brings him closer to the responsibility of the marriageable years. The boy uses this step for the purpose of pursuing forbidden and dangerous games, for which the rhinoceros is the symbol. Yang Hsiung could not avoid condemning this. It is interesting that in the fifth step, the culminating step, there is a negative aspect to the image of the boy.

6. "The curtain is opened widely in order to welcome guests from all directions."

Added commentary: "The curtain is opened widely: an extensive view of all that is bright."

This step, the most intense of the entire tetragram, comes at the beginning of the decline, when the essence of boyhood begins to dissipate. Here the curtain is drawn aside for the initiation celebration, and the guests come with their gifts and teachings.

7. "To cultivate a puppet as if it were a dwarf."

Added commentary: "The cultivation of a puppet is impossible to attain."

The previous step was, however, apparently transitory. We have here an induration of the boyishness into something like a marionette. This step, just like the next one, does not refer to the one being led, but to the leader, who in vain tries to educate the puppet, though, according to Yang Hsiung, Pinocchio cannot become a real boy.[45]

8. "He might beat him, he might spur him. To polish the mysterious mirror would start the flow."

Added commentary: "To beat him and spur him: he is overly decrepit."

Here the educator attempts stronger measures. Meanwhile, however, the mirror of the mystery has become blind in the boy. Thus there is no more help available.

45. This and the next step have been interpreted differently in Chinese literature. Ssu-ma Kuang, for instance, sees in it the infantility of senility.

9. "The fawn gores the buffalo. Its head shatters."

Added commentary: "The fawn gores the buffalo: he returns to self-restriction."

The last step shows the boy, who actively expresses his childlike opposition, and whose head is shattered for this reason. This is not the revolutionary's gesture, which Yang Hsiung does not know, but the gesture of spite. The powerful and comfortable buffalo as an image of the realities the defiant child runs up against does not even have to make use of its horns.[46] The shattered head leads the boy back to the beginning, to the constraint in the self.

Yang Hsiung's appropriate images will have become clear to anyone who is familiar with child psychology. When compared to the texts of the fourth hexagram in the Book of Changes, an essential part of the content appears once again to have been lost in this case. Yang Hsiung does not speak about the success of youth, even of foolish youth. He does not show that the youthful fool as such has qualities denied to those of a more advanced age. Youth's immediacy and its harmony with time, which are so fortunate according to the Book of Changes, are not mentioned by him. There is no place for such ideas about youth in the world of orders and institutions, which is what Yang Hsiung is concerned about.

Yang Hsiung treated another aspect of leadership in the nineteenth tetragram, *Ts'ung*, Following. This tetragram imitates Hexagram 17 of the Book of Changes, *Sui*, Following. Here the text of the tetragram is: "The Yang leaps into the abyss, into the pond, into the fields, onto the mountain peak. The things anxiously observe its pace."

This shows where one can be led when following, again by the yang. It can go into the abyss or up to the mountain peaks, into the serenity of the lake or the toils of the fields. The individual texts in nine steps read:

46. Compare "the sacrament of the Buffalo" in the novel of Heinrich Böll, *Billiard um halb zehn* (Cologne: Kiepenheuer & Witsch, 1959).

1. The sun, still somber, attaches himself to it; the moon, still dark, succeeds it. This is the foundation.

Added commentary: "The sun attaches, the moon succeeds: it is to the foundation that the official responds."

Thus the tetragram begins with the leading of the celestial bodies by a principle unnamed here. This leadership is already effective before the celestial bodies can rise to their function of dispensing light. The subsequent disseminators of spiritual light are the ones led, before they radiate while leading. Significantly, Yang Hsiung compares this phenomenon with the position of the civil servant.

2. "Just coming forth, it is still dawn. Friends follow your kind of acting."

Added commentary: "Just coming forth, the friends follow: they do not know where the path will lead."

Now here there is light, and although it has not yet broken through altogether, the mechanism of leadership begins immediately. The morning's dawn already compels following, a following that does not even necessarily lead to the accomplishment of a known goal.

3. "People do not attack him, they let themselves be led by a rope to follow him."

Added commentary: "People do not attack him: this is the measure of self-acting."

This text recalls six at the top of the seventeenth hexagram, in which the one led also follows, bound (by a rope).[47] The Book of Changes uses here the same word, ts'ung. In the Book of Changes this is the most extreme step of following, in which the one being led is eventually introduced to the leader's ancestors in the sanctuary. In Yang Hsiung this text designates the stage in which inner inhibitions no longer stand in the way of being led, so that being led has turned into a natural attitude.[48]

47. Wilhelm-Baynes, p. 74.
48. The term *self-acting* used above also means "natural."

4. "They cackle while they follow, this is not right. There is a woman holding up a bloody basket. Perdition."

Added commentary: "The perdition of the cackling following: how could one consort with this?"

Here the followers take pride in following. They assume a voice, where they should only follow in a serving position. Yang Hsiung condemns this sharply, because he sees that an element incompatible with following has been interpolated into the situation. The woman with blood in the basket is an allusion to six at the top of the fifty-fourth hexagram in the Book of Changes, where the text reads: "The woman holds the basket, but there are no fruits in it. The man stabs the sheep, but no blood flows. Nothing that acts to further."[49]

The situation underlying this image is the sacrifice of the newlyweds, who are in need of the blessing of the divinity for their recent marriage. The sacrifice is rejected, however; the marriage does not turn into a sacrament. In Yang Hsiung the woman's basket is not empty; it contains blood, which as such is reserved for the sacrifice by the man. The woman successfully usurps the sacred action of the man for herself (whereas in the Book of Changes it is without success), and begins to cackle about it. This must of course appear pernicious to Yang Hsiung.

5. "To follow like water until the hole is filled."

Added commentary: "To follow like water and fill the hole: you do not transcend yourself."

This is our tetragram's step of culmination. Yang Hsiung also used the image of the hole-filling water one time in the *Fa-yen*. There the following passage is found:

> Someone asked Yang Hsiung about progress in an official career. Yang Hsiung said: "You just have to look at flowing water."
>
> The other one said: "You are saying this, are you not, because water does not cease flowing day and night?"

49. Wilhelm-Baynes, p. 212.

Yang Hsiung said: "How can you assume that! It is the water that fills all holes and then runs further."[50]

The highest step of following, which resembles the self-renouncing essence of the water, is also here associated with the career of the civil servant.

6. "They follow their eyes and ignore their stomach."

Added commentary: "To follow one's eye and ignore one's stomach: this is to follow the greed for the exalted."

The following becomes ambitious here. It is no longer an attitude that satisfies in itself, rather it serves as a steppingstone to higher positions. The economic dependency of the one being led, the filling of his stomach, thus is forgotten.

7. "To sweep away what is bad and follow what is pure. Realgar eats away diseased flesh."

Added commentary: "To sweep away what is bad and follow the pure: this is rescue from disaster."

At this step, the second of the descent, it should be noted that initiative is demanded of the follower. The leadership also shows, next to the pure, which can be followed further, the base, which must be expurgated just like diseased flesh. This operation is permissible, since without it harm would not only affect the follower, but would also have general effects. Nevertheless, the follower's situation becomes ambivalent.

8. "To follow the impure. Misfortune is set aflight beyond pursuit."

Added commentary: "To follow the impure: misfortune cannot be corrected by trial."

If an impure leadership is followed without contradiction, then this leads to a catastrophe, which cannot be halted. Of no use then is the defense: I was only following orders.

9. "To follow the eminent, eventually one ascends the steps. This is the final achievement."

50. Zach, p. 3.

Added commentary: "To follow the eminent: eventually one achieves merits."

At the final step following is overcome, the one being led turns into the leader, to whom merits are accorded. Such a positive conclusion of a tetragram is unique. It shows that by means of a self-renouncing acceptance of the proper leadership the end does not run again into the beginning. Rather, it leads to the attainment of a new step.

The images of the corresponding hexagrams in the Book of Changes have already been alluded to once before.[51] Compared with Yang's tetragram, it would be appropriate to exclaim along with Faust:

> How differently upon me works this sign!
> Thou, Spirit of the Earth, I feel, art nigher.[52]

II

This summer we have been charged to investigate once again the import of Eranos.[53] And thus I would like to add a few words that concern me personally as well as my contributions, to that which has been said about Olga Fröbe and about the participants in our meetings. I remember the first summer that I spoke here, and the satisfaction Olga Fröbe expressed to me after my presentation: "Now the Book of Changes has also had a chance to speak to us." For future conferences I have occasionally proposed to treat themes that are based on other areas of Chinese intellectual history and Chinese religion. Olga Fröbe again and again advised me, however: "Stick to the Book of Changes." And when she chose the theme for this year's conference, that of man in service and the leading and

51. See pp. 73–77.
52. Faust I, Scene I, "Night." Priest's translation.
53. This was the first Eranos Meeting after the death of Olga Fröbe.

being led in service, she knew that the Book of Changes also had something to contribute to this theme.

Because for Olga Fröbe, Eranos was a service, not in the sense of laboratory or desk work, where new and operative formulae can be prepared in order to apprehend life and then to classify it, but in the sense of the service in life as a whole, of which the laboratory and the desk are only a part. Moreover, a service in an endangered life, in which life's guiding powers have schizophrenically diverged and have fallen into a nonsensical civil war. At this stage one part attempts to rule the other by means of rational orders and temporal institutions, so that life is in danger of being deprived of its fullness. In the presence of this danger, Olga Fröbe established Eranos, not for the purpose of seeking new formulae that could be set against the prevailing ones, but as a manifestation of life's wholeness. Man's service constitutes this manifestation, since he is leader as well as the one led. In this way the high pretensions of Eranos and its humility are manifested.

The Book of Changes advances a similar demand, of a type that expresses itself in a similar humility. It does not attempt to impose an order upon life, but it sees man in service, a service that occurs in tensive relation to life's wholeness. Within this relation to wholeness, man's service is but one of the powers that keep life in a state of flux, and the spirit is only one part of man. Man is the leader and the one led. He is led, however, not solely by man and not only by rational orders and temporal institutions, which the human spirit with its ulterior motives and its ambition has imposed upon life. Instead, man in service is viewed as a member of the great trinity: heaven, earth, and man.

If we now wish to turn our attention to the interaction of these three powers, it appears superficially to correspond to an unrealistic and almost escapist attitude. We appear to regress one step if we once again devote our attention to the Book of Changes, especially

[151]

after Yang Hsiung has shown the power of rational orders and temporal institutions, and after he sought to render in his system a dominating expression to this power, which we cannot fail to recognize. This step backwards, however, means the same thing as the establishment of Eranos: only in this way are we able to escape the confinement in the system of orders and institutions, and only thus can we again recognize life in its wholeness. It is a step out of confinement into freedom. Within the system of orders and institutions, whose dominating influence none of us can deny, Yang Hsiung's words may have something of significance and of ingenuity to say to us. However, we can only recognize the system as such and its meaning if we take this step backwards. Just like Eranos, we tread here in all humility and with high pretensions.

The Book of Changes does not offer any hard and fast formulae for the interaction of heaven, earth, and man. In every situation the cooperation and collaboration, and even occasionally the opposition of the three powers operate differently. The familiar words of the T'uan Commentary to Hexagram 15, *Ch'ien*, Modesty, express this interplay:

> It is the way of heaven to shed its influence downward and to create light and radiance. It is the way of the earth to be lowly and to go upward.
>
> It is the way of heaven to make empty what is full and to give increase to what is modest. It is the way of the earth to change the full and to augment the modest. . . . It is the way of men to hate fullness and to love the modest.[54]

This is an example. In every point of what the Book of Changes calls "the confused diversities," this interplay operates differently. This implies that the qualities of the three powers are in no way of a fixed or exclusive nature. As a rule heaven is of course the creative, and the earth is the preserving and the formative. Occasionally, heaven is then the form-giving and that which embodies the "law

54. Wilhelm-Baynes, p. 462.

under which you were born," and earth is that which resists perfection in form. In other passages this perfection is based on an
interaction of heaven and earth, and in the T'uan Commentary to
Hexagram 22, Pi, Grace, this consummating form is the work of
man.[55] Man's role is therefore in no way given once and for all.
Cases are numerous in which he is to be in accordance with heaven
and must follow the earth. However, there are also cases where he
anticipates heaven, and yet heaven does not oppose him. And then
there are other cases, in which man follows heaven, and he must
be in accordance with "men." Thus it is under the sign of Revolution, in which the success of the great revolutionaries of the past is
attributed to their being submissive toward heaven and in accord
with man,[56] and under the sign of the Joyous, where, if one submits
to heaven and is in accord with man, drudgery and even death lose
their sting.[57]

The three powers, which confront us here in their diverse constellations of interplay, reached their complete development only
in the later strata of the Book of Changes. In the earlier strata it is
easier to recognize them by their effects than by their essence.
There heaven is still the name for the highest deity, a name the
early Chou had in common with other peoples who came up out of
the steppes.

Earth is the primordial, often uncanny power of the arable soil,
in its turn the keeper of souls that have returned to the eternal
night.[58]

Only the exalted amongst men stood in contact with the god of
heaven and the power of earth. A particular charisma was required
to bring oneself into accord with heaven and earth through sac-

55. Ibid., p. 495.
56. Ibid., p. 636.
57. Ibid., p. 686.
58. See Henri Maspero, *Mélanges posthumes sur les religions et l'histoire de
le Chine* (Paris, 1950), p. 204.

rifice or prayer. The book's later strata have secularized these essentially religiously experienced powers; in the case of the earth they have even substituted a new word, which also realizes the spread-out polymorphism in the element of the earth (soil), by means of the added image of the snake. But even these secularized concepts still include the numinous of prehistory; they have not yet become the spiritual tools of artisans, as in Yang Hsiung. The mysterious contiguity of heaven and earth, which creates things, is still there. This enduring experience found its most beautiful expression in the sentence: "The greatest virtue of heaven and earth is to live."

Man, above all the working and creating man, is now confronted by these concepts, which still partake of the divine. Here, too, the terminology that characterizes man is more developed and more discriminating in the later strata. The later strata know the saint, he who has a direct contact with divine powers and therefore can speak with authority about the appropriate and about man's position within the appropriate. The later strata also know the sage, who often lives in seclusion and is frequently without a suitable worldly position; who, however, despite these restraints, embodies permanence in his nature, and reaches towards greatness in his actions. And finally, they know the superior man, who finds the proper path in every single presenting situation, and thus grants to man leadership and a model.

The earlier strata of the book are not acquainted with all these types, and wherever they appear in our present texts it can now be shown that we have an interpolation. Instead of this, the earlier strata are familiar with the dark man, the *homo teneber* (the man from the shadows), who is at home in the dark valley of the mothers. The dark valley as the mothers' domicile is a mythological image, which the Book of Changes has in common with the Book of Songs and with Lao-tse's *Tao-te-ching*. The dark valley appears in the Book of Changes as the place of gloom,[59] into which one strays if one gives in to despair. In the Book of Songs it appears as the place from which one emerges strengthened into a new life. The dark man, however, the inhabitant of this valley, is characterized in the Book of Changes by his perseverance. He salutarily assists anyone who, when following, pursues a level course modestly and without a specific goal; when, in other words, following is not a purposeful striving, but rather an unconscious attitude.[60] And he assists the girl abandoned by her companions, who therefore has to follow her own light alone;[61] to whom it can be shown that the permanent law still remains unchanged in her solitude. In both cases the dark man is the representative of the Great Mother, submitting to whom can lead one into a state of oppressive despair, but whose representative renders the power of perseverance to the one being led and to the lonely person.

Other human types who play a role in the older texts are not necessarily called to exercise leadership. We find here, for example, the wanderer, to whom an entire hexagram is dedicated,[62] who essentially traverses his meandering path alone, and whose traveling only occasionally is enlivened by a companion. We find the citizen, who willingly follows the king's leadership,[63] but whose property is in no way protected;[64] we find the soldier, who must willingly sacrifice himself for his prince,[65] and—be it advancing or retreating—must remain tenaciously faithful to his goal;[66] we find the hero (the strong man), to whom the army is indebted for

59. Hex. 47, 6/1, Wilhelm-Baynes, pp. 625–26.
60. Hex. 10, 9/2, ibid., p. 437.
61. Hex. 54, 9/2, ibid., p. 666.
62. Hex. 56. On him see pp. 180–86.
63. Hex. 8, 9/5, Wilhelm-Baynes, p. 429.
64. Hex. 25, 6/3, ibid., p. 512.
65. Hex. 10, 6/3, ibid., p. 438.
66. Hex. 57, 6/1, ibid., p. 681.

leadership,[67] but who can also get into an ambivalent rivalry with the little boy.[68]

Aside from these human types, who are characterized by their occupation and by their nature, the older strata know two other types of a more general kind, who are simply designated as "the great man" and the "little man." In their case the problem of leadership becomes particularly clear. Already, from the types enumerated, it follows that leading and being led by man comes into play only rarely, and that man, active or suffering, usually travels his path alone. This is strikingly evident in the figure of the little man, a type we should assume to be in particular need of leadership and thus to be open to it. In the ten texts in the older strata in which the little man is discussed, he receives a share of such leadership in only one. This occurs in the six in the fifth place in Hexagram 40, *Hsieh*, Deliverance,[69] where the liberator achieves deliverance, and in his sincerity lets the little man partake in the fruits of deliverance. Only a superficial imitation occurs in other cases, as for example in the six at the top of Hexagram 49, where the little man, confronted with pantherlike developments, merely molts his face.[70] In other cases the little man is a person who is not able to cope with a situation, and as a consequence is repudiated or falls into disaster, even if the same situation and even the same type of action would still yield good fortune and reward to stronger personalities. It is expressed twice,[71] that the little man is to be neglected, whenever investitures and rewards are allotted upon the victorious conclusion of a campaign. It is said once that the little man does not qualify when a prince introduces his helpers to the Son of Heaven.[72] If the little man wants to exploit his power, he

67. Hex. 7, Judgment, ibid., p. 421.
68. Hex. 17, 6/2 and 6/3, ibid., p. 474.
69. Cf. ibid., p. 588.
70. Ibid., p. 640.
71. Hex. 7, 6/6 ibid., p. 424, and Hex. 63, 9/3, ibid., p. 712.
72. Hex. 14, 9/3, ibid., p. 459.

is compared to a goat that butts against the hedge and gets its horns entangled.[73] If he retreats voluntarily, a mode of behavior that brings good fortune and advantage to others, it brings downfall to the little man.[74] And when others still receive booty from the remainders of Splitting Apart, the little man's last resort is split apart, namely his house.[75]

The fate of the little man is to bear and to endure. If he, however, accepts this fate, it means good fortune for the little man, while the same attitude would bring about the downfall of the great man.[76] Then there are insights given to the little man that remain concealed from others. The six at the beginning of Hexagram 20, *Kuan*, Contemplation, has the lines: "Boylike contemplation. For a little man, no blame."[77]

The unselfconscious, unreflected, even uncomprehending contemplation is open here only to the little man. Such a contemplation eventually makes him, too, capable of accomplishing great deeds.[78] And if he advances on this path, then he will finally be led to a contemplation of his own life and of life in general.

It is striking how little leadership is given the little man, the one who endures and who is discriminated against. In general, also, the little man has to stand on his own feet. The difference of the times becomes especially clear, if we hold these texts next to those of Yang Hsiung, in which the leader and the one being led have institutionally determined positions, in which the rejection of leadership is understood as guilt and the consequences of unled action are seen as punishment.

In the texts of the Book of Changes, although leadership is never offered, it is sometimes sought: "It is not I who seek the young

73. Hex. 34, 9/3, ibid., p. 558.
74. Hex. 33, 9/4, ibid., p. 553.
75. Hex. 23, 9/6, ibid., p. 503.
76. Hex. 12, 6/2, ibid., p. 449.
77. Ibid., p. 487.
78. See Hex. 42, 9/1, ibid., p. 598.

fool;/The young fool seeks me," is in the Judgment of the fourth hexagram.[79] And it is at this place that the field of action opens itself for the great man. The great man is nowhere designated as leader; the nature of his influence nowhere described. In a series of situations, however, it is advised to search for the great man with the words: "It furthers one to see the great man."

The word that my father, Richard Wilhelm, has translated here as "to see" is an extremely weighty, even solemn word. It is also used in early texts whenever one wants to be admitted to an audience with his prince. In the phrase *to see* by itself it is thus expressed that advice is being respectfully sought.

It may be of interest to envisage the cases in which the advice and leadership of the great man are furthering. These are infrequent cases, and it is not to be expected otherwise, because only a frugal use should be made of the relationship to the great man.

Seeing the great man is, to begin with, indicated in several unfortunate situations, in which dealing on one's own with the prevailing relationships would be difficult. For example, this is the case in Hexagram 39, *Chien*, Obstruction, which shows the image of the dangerous abyss on top of the mountain. Here it is said in the Judgment: "It furthers one to see the great man. Perseverance brings good fortune.[80]

If the images of this hexagram are followed, then retreat is indicated in the presence of this dizzying view, since the obstruction is of a type that cannot be mastered by direct assault. However, the retreat is not a flight from danger, but a retreat into oneself, a time in which one's own being and one's own power will be developed. Such a retreat is indicated, even if the obstructions are not evoked by one's own inadequacies, or if they are attributable to external relationships, even institutional relations, and not to one's own guilt. Then the constellation turns, the obstructions are over-

79. Ibid., pp. 406–7.
80. Ibid., p. 580.

come, and once again there is forward progress. In the strongest line of the hexagram, the nine in the fifth place, this overcoming occurs in the midst of the greatest obstructions, due to the coming of friends.

This danger lies in an exaggerated concentration on oneself, where one might be tempted to place interest in oneself ahead of interest in the service. It is once again seen as an obstruction, even though a different type of obstruction. This situation is shown in the six at the top whose text reads: "Going leads to obstructions, coming leads to great good fortune. It furthers one to see the great man."[81]

The position of the line demonstrates that the external obstructions have already been overcome, the work has thus already been done. To continue to be occupied with oneself creates a new obstruction, which must once again be overcome, again with the aid of the great man, who leads the perplexed one to transcend his self-concern and to set himself once again to serve. It may be remarked that the texts of this hexagram have an exquisite formal beauty. Rhythm and rhyme give them a compactness found occasionally in line texts, and which has here an impact on the unconscious just like a beautiful and affecting song; in its magic it can help to induce the correct psychological attitude, by means of which obstructions can be overcome.

A further case in which the great man should be sought is Hexagram 6, *Sung*, Conflict, in which the creating heaven is opposed to the dangerous, tearing water. Here the Judgment reads: "Be sincere even if you are smothered and are lying on the ground. In the middle, good fortune, at the end, misfortune. It furthers one to see the great man. It does not further one to cross the great water."[82]

Here we see the powerful heaven as one of the parties in the

81. Ibid., p. 583.
82. Ibid., p. 416. I differ here somewhat from my father's translation.

[159]

conflict. It strangles its opponent and throws him to the ground. It can only be a misfortune for both sides to carry this conflict through to the bitter end. The solution would be to stop in the middle. But in this situation of conflict, neither of the two is capable of such a solution on his own. The great man's advice may bring such a solution about, a solution that once again releases the powers of the conflicting parties from the unfortunate battle. It is not yet, however, the time to proceed to action.

There are also cases of a much more favorable constellation, in which it may be advisable to see the great man. Such a case, for example, is present in Hexagram 45, *Ts'ui*, Gathering Together, in which the king gathers the powers of his people in order to lead his nation towards great achievements; and he sanctions this gathering by means of a religious act. The text of the Judgment reads here:

> Gathering together. Success. The king approaches his temple. It furthers one to see the great man. This brings success. Perseverance furthers. To bring great offerings creates good fortune. It furthers one to undertake something.[83]

We cannot pursue here this hexagram's individual aspects. It is one of the richest in excitement in the entire book. The situation here is ready for the great undertaking. The achievement is of such import that a religious sanction seems to be indicated. However, one should see the great man here even before the performance of the offering, because it is to be feared that the great offering, the religious sanction as such, will overshadow and conceal the complex relations, which are brought to life by the sheer size of the action. Among these relations and consequences there are many that in no way have gratifying aspects, even though the achievement as such leads to great good fortune. It can only be accomplished through the blood and bitter tears of those called to

83. Ibid., pp. 614–15.

gather together. A religious sanction, which conceals such results, could deny success to the achievement. Therefore it is furthering to be instructed by the great man, before the offering is executed.

An almost diametrically opposed situation is found in Hexagram 57, *Sun*, The Gentle. Here the gentle but unceasing influence of the wind is shown, the persistent effect in miniature. The text of the Judgment reads here: "The Gentle. Success through what is small. It furthers one to have somewhere to go. It furthers one to see the great man." [84]

The danger here is that persistent action on a small scale becomes diffuse, that it is aligned to acting as such, without reference to a goal. The constant blowing of the wind, constant occupation, which devotes itself aimlessly to work as such and thus loses sight of the work's end, does not necessarily lead to success; it can lead to confusion and to the loss of what is essential. To persist in work in such a manner brings misfortune. And it is once again the great man who places a firm goal out in front, a goal one can work toward without losing oneself in diffusion.

Perhaps the most interesting, however, are the lines in Hexagram 1, *Ch'ien*, The Creative, in which it appears to be indicated to see the great man. One would be inclined to assume that the creative man can do without the help of the great man. People inferior in status have been charged to complete their work on their own. It seems surprising that in certain cases the creative man is in need of leadership. We nevertheless find the advice to see the great man not only in one place, but expressed in two places of the first hexagram, at the nine in the second place, the dragon appearing in the field, and at the nine in the fifth place, the flying dragon in the heavens. [85]

The second nine shows one of the most tragic points in the development of the creative man. It is the time when his genius

84. Ibid., p. 680.
85. Ibid., pp. 373, 374.

appears for the first time, in the field to be sure, and not raised above his contemporaries. Here he remains caught in the pragmatic; he lacks the ability to rise beyond the place of his origin, the waters of the deep. He turns into a domesticated genius, and time finally passes him by. The help of the great man is required, in order to support him in such a tragic situation.

Even more surprising is the advice of the nine in the fifth place, the case of the flying dragon in the heavens, the place where the creative has attained its majestic culmination. The rise above the waters of the deep has succeeded; a new field of action, the world of heaven, is gained. In this situation the great man's help is necessary, the help of a man who sees each position in a cosmic connection, so that such success does not lead to tragic hybris. The humility demanded here from the creative man borders on the impossible. Who does not know the mental attitude of a successful creative genius? This position cannot, however, be maintained without just such an extreme humility at the moment of highest success. Veracity and affability must be allied with dignity, or, quoting verbatim: "Only the help of the great man can bring about the highest success of the creative without the loss of integrity."[86] With this we have skimmed over the cases in which having an audience with the great man is indicated. We have seen that his leadership takes effect in relations of the most diverse type, but also that men of the most diverse natures permit themselves to be led by him: the obstructed one, the one beaten in conflict, the king on the eve of the great work, the one preoccupied with persistent detail, and in conclusion, the creative genius. In the Book of Changes the action of the great man is once called "creating,"[87] a word that as a rule is applied to the divinity or to heaven in their acts of creation, such as in the sentence: "Heaven creates from chaos and darkness."

86. Hex. 14, 6/5, cf. ibid., p. 460.
87. Hex. 1, 9/5, Little Image.

The secret of the great man's effectiveness is nowhere described in the Book of Changes, as has been stated earlier. However, the origin of this effectiveness is indicated in the sentence that reads: "This great man; his character accords with heaven and earth."[88]

We have seen before that the greatest virtue of heaven and earth is to live. To form life and form within life, a man is required, in whom the harmony of the great trinity is embodied.

However, we have also seen that the leadership of such a man is appealed to only infrequently. In only five of the sixty-four cases does one go to an audience with the great man, and this only under certain circumstances; in the remaining fifty-nine, man has to stand on his own, and he must do without this human leadership. He cannot let himself be guided by human orders and temporal institutions, as in Yang Hsiung's world. Compensating for this, however, the book provides him with leadership, or at least with a clue as to the manner in which this leadership can be attained. It says in the Great Treatise:

> Looking upward, we contemplate with its help the signs in the heavens; looking down, we examine the lines of the earth. Thus we come to know the circumstances of the dark and the light. Going back to the beginnings of things and pursuing them to the end, we come to know the lessons of birth and of death. . . .
>
> Since in this way man comes to resemble heaven and earth, he is not in conflict with them. His wisdom embraces all things, and his Tao brings order into the whole world; therefore he does not err. He is active everywhere but does not let himself be carried away. He rejoices in heaven and has knowledge of fate, therefore he is free of care. He is content with his circumstances and genuine in his kindness, therefore he can practice love.[89]

In man, who is exalted here in a manner seldom found elsewhere in literature, in each man and not only in the great man, the interaction of heaven, earth, and man thus comes to pass.

88. Cf. Wilhelm-Baynes, p. 382.
89. Ibid., pp. 294–95.

VI

WANDERINGS OF THE SPIRIT

In that part of the United States where I have my home, we are treated every autumn to a powerful spectacle: the spawning of the salmon. Our cabin stands at the concourse of a little brook, French Creek, and the Stillaguamish, one of the rivers that carry the glacial waters of the Cascade Mountains. Usually the spawning begins in September, at a time when river and creek run low. School on school, the great fish come, swimming upstream in their battle against the current and tearing rapids. Often these are hard to conquer. The fish summons its entire strength in working itself up through the rapids, and is seldom successful on the first attempt. The fish tries again and again, and is often so exhausted that when at last it succeeds, the current pulls it down again. Many remain lying in eddies, food for the bears; others succeed finally, and then they wait again, school on school, at the mouth of the creek, till a little rain partially refills the nearly dried-up bed.

Then the battle begins afresh, up the narrow, shallow, and often precipitous creek bed, to find the place whence they sprang, in order to give themselves to the business of spawning. They arrive there battered and bruised and end their life cycle with this action.

Theodore Roethke, in his cycle of poems, *Meditations of an Old Woman*, built the following image:

So the spirit tries for another life,
Another way and place in which to continue;
Or a salmon, tired, moving up a shallow stream,
Nudges into a back-eddy, a sandy inlet,
Bumping against sticks and bottom-stones, then swinging
Around, back into the maincurrent, the rush of brownish-white water,
Still swimming forward—
So, I suppose, the spirit journeys.[1]

Wanderings of the spirit on the lookout for another life, for continuing in another way, and place, have frequently been described in early Chinese literature. Such descriptions represent an attempt to surmount the constraints of the existing world by a flight into the world of ideas. The word *idea* is to be understood here in its original meaning, not as a mirror of the existing world or a reflection into the existing world, but as a view and a viewed image.

In the early Chinese sketches of such trips into the world of ideas, this world appears as a view of the spirit whose figures and settings are taken from mythical images and images from the ecstatic experiences of shamans.[2] They are images made visible in the religious tradition, and in religious experience, images in which strata of fateful participation are portrayed, fantasies, therefore, and imaginings that the mind perceived and projected out of the self into the universe.

In the age we are discussing here, encompassing, as we count time, the last centuries B.C. and the first centuries A.D., the Chinese mind was completely at home in these worlds of fantasy and imagi-

1. Theodore Roethke, *The Collected Poems* (New York: Doubleday, 1966), p. 159.
2. See Mircea Eliade, *Shamanism* (New York: Pantheon Books, 1964), pp. 448–61.

nation. Wanderings and experiences in these worlds had a thoroughly familiar quality. This world of the mind's view was not opposed to the world of so-called real existence to the degree that one could only visit it in shyness and awe. More than in the existing world one could move about here as a *homo ludens*, playfully and without embarrassment. Moreover, it was a world in which embarrassment had no place, a world into which one lifted oneself out of conditioned and conditioning entanglements. Close relationships to the gods and goddesses and fairies were given, and free use was made of their institutions and habits.

An early sketch of such a wandering of the spirit is provided by the poet Ch'ü Yüan (late fourth and early third century B.C.). Ch'ü Yüan was a member of the royal court of one of the Chinese southern states, Ch'u, and as such was also involved in politics. He could not approve of the specific politics of his royal relative; he could foresee that these policies would lead to misfortune for the king himself as well as for the state.

History proved him right; but before that happened he had fallen under a cloud for admonishing the court. He fell victim to slander and was finally banished. This fate hit him doubly hard, it ruined his own life and bode ill for the future of his country. He gave expression to his despair in a long poem. This is the *Li Sao*, which could be translated as "Encountering Sorrow."[3]

Here the poet comes to a decision, after a poetic description of the adverse circumstances of his life, to go upon a wandering of the spirit. He gives himself up to the insight that the world of entanglements has no more room for him, but that the doors stand open to his spirit. For how could even dismemberment, says he, ever hurt my spirit? His girl playmates try in vain to lure him away

3. There are several translations of the *Li Sao*. The latest and best is that of David Hawkes, *Ch'u Tz'u: The Songs of the South* (Oxford: Clarendon Press, 1959), pp. 21–34. On the traditions concerning Ch'ü Yüan's life, see pp. 11–16.

from his decision. "You have us for companions, who can know your spirit," they call to him.

Withstanding these enticements, he hitches the jade dragons to his phoenix carriage and a favorable wind carries him upon his journey. Having taken leave in the morning, he arrives in the evening at the garden of paradise (literally, the hanging gardens of K'un-lun). There he stops the sun, that he may enjoy its beauties longer. Then his flight continues. The god of the wind is his outrider, the heavenly bird his herald, and the god of thunder his executor.

Station after station pass in fantastic images and finally he undertakes the search for the fairy who can bring him comfort. He meets several: the River Goddess of the Lo River, who is too frivolous to suit him, the Ancestress of the House of Shang, who is too reserved—even the intercession of the magpie does not help—and then the two Princesses Yü, whom he cannot wake from sleep. After these failures he is granted an oracle that promises him the most beautiful one of all.

The journey to her is long, drawn out, and colorful. He is finally able to designate the western ocean as their meeting place. He orders his thousand wagons prepared, hub of jade on hub of jade they fly along, side by side, pulled by dragons, his cloud-rimmed banners fluttering in the breeze. Already the final joy seems in his grasp when suddenly he looks down from the magnificence of the heavens and sees his old home. His groom's heart grows heavy, his horses arch their heads with longing and refuse to go on.

It is not difficult to perceive that this flight is an attempt to escape and, moreover, an unsuccessful attempt. Not long after completing the poem Ch'ü Yüan himself ended his life. The entanglements from which his spirit wanted to escape caught up with him in the end.

The reason for this is not hard to understand. On his wandering,

Ch'ü Yüan encountered the schism between the image and its meaning, between vision and allegory. On his journey of the spirit he did not escape worldly meaning. The allegory of sensual union, according to the Book of Changes, was often used in order to allude to the relationship between ruler and advisor. What Ch'ü Yüan was looking for on this journey was not perceived and pursued joy, anticipated and enjoyed unaffectedly; it was a symbol of his lost worldly position. As an aristocrat and patriot, dignity lay close to his heart—the dignity of his person as well as that of his home state.

This is strongly expressed in his poem. To keep his dignity, he enters upon his journey. But then the insight comes to him that he cannot escape from himself. The poem ends here; in actual life, however, he took the last step.

Ch'ü Yüan became a hero of Chinese folk legends very early. One of the most beautiful yearly Chinese festivals is associated with his name. This is the Dragonboat Festival, during which a symbolic attempt is made to fish his corpse out of the water in which he drowned himself. Fantastic boat competitions have remained customary to the present day.

All love for his person notwithstanding, Ch'ü Yüan's poetic attempt and his way out did not remain without contradiction. On the one hand, his attempt at flight as such was damned. This was done by Yang Hsiung, in a poem entitled *Fan Li Sao, Anti-Li Sao*.[4] On the other hand many were not convinced by his half-hearted attempt to project a worldly meaning into a vision of the spirit. If one wishes to leave the world and go upon a voyage of the spirit, this can be done only if the worldly meaning is also forgotten. The journey may not be a flight to which traces of the life one has

4. On Yang Hsiung see *Eranos Jahrbuch 1961* 31 (1962):317–37; pp. 126–31, above, and David R. Knechtges, *The Han Rhapsody: A Study of the Fu of Yang Hsiung* (London: Cambridge University Press, 1976).

fled still adhere. Such a journey sets a new goal that has nothing to do with old entanglements. The landscapes of the spirit must become autonomous, and one must give oneself to the newly encountered ideas, completely unprejudiced.

This insight was carried out in a somewhat later poem, which perhaps still belongs to the third century B.C., but whose author is no longer known. This is the *Yüan-yu*, "The Far Off Journey."[5] Here also, the author begins with a lament about worldly conditions in which he finds himself:

> In the night-time I lay, wide-eyed, without sleeping;
> My unquiet soul was active until the daylight.[6]

Then a legendary immortal, Wang Ch'iao, visits him and teaches him how he may achieve immortality, and thereupon the author goes on his journey. The landscapes of the spirit through which he travels very much resemble Ch'ü's, and frequently they are taken literally out of Ch'ü's poem. In contrast to Ch'ü Yüan, he has no difficulties finding goddesses and fairies, listening to their music, and watching their dances.

He leaves them, however, and travels on through the Gate of Coldness to the Spring of Purity, until he finally arrives at the Great Abyss. He looks down, but what he sees is of another kind:

> In the sheer depths below, the earth was invisible;
> In the vastness above, the sky could not be seen.
> When I looked, my startled eyes saw nothing;
> When I listened, no sound met my amazed ear.
> Transcending Inaction, I came to Purity,
> And entered the neighborhood of the Great Beginning.[7]

5. Translated by Hawkes, *Ch'u Tz'u*, pp. 81–87. F. X. Biallas still takes this poem to be one written by Ch'ü Yüan personally; see his "K'ü Yüan's 'Fahrt in die Ferne,' " in *Asia Major* 4 (1927) :51–107; 7 (1932) :179–241. This opinion is no longer shared.

6. Hawkes's translation.

7. Ibid.

We, at Eranos, from other circles of culture, are familiar with the great beginning that emerges from nothingness.[8] Every worldly entanglement is sloughed off here. In freedom from the traces of worldliness, even Taoistic inaction is transcended.

In this poem the shaman has already stepped into the background. His place in the following era is frequently taken over by the alchemist, as here by Wang Ch'iao (or Wang Tzu-ch'iao) who was reputed to have achieved immortality. The trend toward achievement of immortality through spiritual exercises but also by alchemical practices was widespread in those days. More and more it was only the immortal who was capable of such a wandering of the spirit. This thought led to a new genre in Chinese poetry, poems with the title "Wanderings of the Immortals." In them alchemists and magicians have their say. Among the authors can also be found poets who absorbed the imagery of alchemists and their insights of the spirit without adhering to their practices.

Among the earliest poets who used this new genre, Ts'ao Chih (192–232 A.D.) stands out.[9] He too was a prince, a younger son of Ts'ao Ts'ao, who virtually took over the power of the expiring Han Dynasty, and the younger brother of Ts'ao P'i, who established the new Wei Dynasty. All members of the Ts'ao family were poets above the ordinary and concerned themselves with furthering poets and poetry of the era. Ts'ao Chih was one whose poetic genius by far outweighed his political ambitions and who therefore drew the enmity and persecution of his royal relatives. So he too was among the insulted and injured, and he frequently gave complaining expression of this fate in his poetry. He escaped this fate in those poems that deal with the wanderings of the immortals. Two examples can be cited as proof of this:

8. See Gerschom Scholem, "Schöpfung aus Nichts und Selbstverschränkung Gottes," in *Eranos Jahrbuch 1956* 25 (1957) :87–119.

9. See Stephen Shih-tsung Wang, "Tsaur Jyr's Poems of Mythical Excursions." Master's thesis, University of California, Berkeley, 1959.

WANDERINGS OF THE SPIRIT

Ascending to the Heavens I

I don my magic sandals and follow the magician
Far off to P'eng Lai Mountain.
On the magic waters fly up purewhite waves;
The Orchids and Cassia reach up to the sky.
Dark panthers roam down below;
Soaring cranes play up on top.
Riding the wind I am suddenly wafted up,
And seem to see hosts of immortals.[10]

Ballad of the Immortals

The Immortals, holding the dice-sticks,[11]
Sit gaming in a fold of T'ai Mountain.
The Hsiang Goddess strikes her zither;
The Maid of Ch'in blows her pipes;
Cinnamon wine brims in jade cups;
The River Lord serves sacred fish.
The Four Seas are too cramped for me;
In the world's Nine Lands I have nowhere to go.
But Han Chung and Wang Ch'iao[12]
Wait for me in the sky's crossroads.
Ten-thousand leagues is nothing!
Lightly I vault through space
And leaping, soar over argent clouds.
A high wind blows my body onward,
And round I drift to see Heaven's starry palace
And match my tally with Heaven's king.
The Gate of God's City rises sheer,
The gate-towers ten-thousand fathoms tall.

10. Translation by George W. Kent in *Worlds of Dust and Jade* (New York: Philosophical Library, 1969), p. 80.

11. A game with six sticks that immortals and fairies like to play. Mortals, also, can master it and if ever they win against an immortal partner they receive as a prize his magic powers. See Yang Lien-sheng, "A Note on the So-Called TLV Mirrors and the Game Liu-po," *Harvard Journal of Asian Studies* 9:202–6 and 15:124–39.

12. Two sages who obtained immortality through the use of magical elixirs.

[171]

Jade trees line the road to it;
White tigers guard its doors. . . .[13]

The attempt to transcend worldly entanglements in imaginary wanderings and to describe those wanderings poetically was thereafter frequently undertaken. The realization soon came, however, that such wanderings are fantasies (wish-dreams) that the human spirit can well imagine but cannot consummate. The idea of the spirit fettered to life, specifically individual life, established itself more and more in the center of awareness. The concern was then one of transcending material fetters in life itself, and this drew the exercises and recipes of alchemy into the picture, their goal was to conquer the fetters of the body and thereby to set the spirit free.

Here we might mention Hsi K'ang (223–262 A.D.), a Taoist philosopher, alchemist, and sensitive poet,[14] whose pursuit of immortality, however, was terminated by the executioner's sword because he defended a politically unpopular friend. We are indebted to him for a "Treatise Concerning the Nourishment of Life," in which he analyzes alchemistic possibilities. Towards the end of this treatise he says:

> . . . If one is good at nourishing life, then he is not thus! He is pure and void, tranquil and expansive; his ego is small and his desires few. Knowing that reputation and rank injure power, he therefore takes them lightly and makes no plans for them. This is not a case of first desiring something and then suppressing it. Knowing that good eating harms the basic nature, he therefore casts it out and does not care for it. This is not being greedy while later suppressing it. Because external affairs bind

13. Translated by David Hawkes in *The Far East: China and Japan*, ed. Douglas Grant and Millar Maclure (Toronto: University of Toronto Press, 1961), pp. 320–21.

14. On him, see Donald Holzman, *La vie et la pensée de Hsi K'ang* (Leiden: E. J. Brill, 1957), and Jerry Swanson, "Hsi K'ang and His Yang-sheng Lun" in *Studies in Philosophy and in the History of Science: Essays in Honor of Max Frisch*, ed. R. Tursman (Lawrence, Kansas: Coronado Press, 1970), pp. 136–58.

the mind, he does not dwell on them. Spiritual power, because it is pure and pristine, is alone manifest in him. He is expansive and has no anxieties nor crises; he is still; he has no thoughts nor worries. Moreover he protects himself with the unity; he nourishes himself with harmony. The principle of this harmony daily becomes more apparent and he is in tune with the Great Concord. Only then can he steam himself with the *ling-chih* plant and drink the unfermented wine, only then can he pacify himself with the five musical strings of the zither. He does nothing, yet is self-content. His body is wonderful; his mind mysterious. He loses himself in joy, yet later his happiness is sufficient. He abandons life, while in the end the body is preserved. Proceeding like this he can easily compare in age to Hsien-men and quarrel about years with Wang Tzu-ch'iao. How can it be that he does not exist?[15]

But before this point is reached, wanderings of the spirit cannot lead to actual liberation. Thus his poem "Wanderings of the Immortals" ends in a resigned rather than hopeful vein. In the ending verses he says:

Give me the spontaneous way,
I would extend as if developing youthful folly.[16]
I would collect herbs in the crags of Mount Chung,
And such nourishment would transform my countenance.
Like the cicada, I would discard entanglements.
I would leave my friends and would make a wooden shack my home.
In front of a jar of wine I would play the Nine Tunes,[17]
And my songs would reverberate into the distance.
After a long separation from the people of the world
Who would still be able to discover my traces?

Even for poets who more successfully evaded worldly entanglements this transposition into the subjunctive mood remained. Ho Shao (who died 301 A.D.), for instance, a Taoist philosopher of the

15. Swanson's translation.
16. A quote from *I ching*, Hex. 4, 6/1 (Wilhelm-Baynes, p. 22).
17. The music of the legendary Emperor Shun referred to in *Lieh-tzu, chüan* 3; see A. C. Graham, *The Book of Lieh-tzu* (London: I. Murray, 1960), p. 62.

following generation, was enough of a loner to make his way among the cliques of his day without bodily harm. His poem "Wanderings of the Immortals" reads:

> In darkest green the pine tree on the hill,
> And elevated high, the cypress on the peak.
> Their sparkling color glows in winter as in summer,
> Their deep roots know how to resist all withering.
> A man of good will has a steadfast heart,
> Looking at things, he longs to be away.
> He strives to fly up to the high dark cloudbank
> And lets his eyes sweep over craggy mountains.
> How happy once was Wang Tzu-ch'iao,
> Soaring with traveling friends high over China's lands.
> Their flight was high above the mountain ranges.
> They unified their wing-sweep like the wandering cranes.
> Ten-thousand miles they flew, what meaning
> For them had all the little joys of man?
> Often I long for the way of these immortals.
> My heart grows wide as if it wished to fly.[18]

More and more "the way of these immortals" disappears from the world of imagination into the world of longing. The topography of these imaginary worlds was well known to everybody in those days; but the unselfconsciousness with which one ascended into those worlds was disappearing. The well-known interpreter of the *I ching*, Kuo P'u (227–324 A.D.), expressed this in his life and in his poetry with special vigor. At his time, the warlord Wang Tun planned a rebellion and demanded Kuo's prognosis for his plans. Kuo predicted failure. Whereupon Wang asked him: "Since you know the future so well, tell, how long will your own life last?" Kuo answered: "It will end today."

---

18. Another translation is in Ilse Fang, ed., E. von Zach, trans., *Die chinesische Anthologie*, Harvard-Yenching Institute Series, study no. 18 (Cambridge, Mass.: Harvard University Press, 1958), 1:327.

Kuo P'u was accurate in both statements. Wang Tun, in his rage, had him executed on the spot.

In his poem "Wanderings of the Immortals," Kuo says:

> How can the Six Dragons[19] be stopped?
> The flow of fate has its ups and downs,
> And the changes of time influence the thought of men.
> If it is autumn you love to think back to the summer.
> In the Huai and in the Ocean little birds are changed,[20]
> My life alone is not transformed.
> Even though it is my wish to ascend to the Cinnabar Valley,
> Clouds and dragons do not serve me as a vehicle.
> I am ashamed not to possess the powers of Lu-yang
> Who was able to turn back the sun by three degrees.
> Sitting at the river bank I regret the passing of the years,
> I stroke my heart and sigh in solitude.[21]

We have to return to our salmon now and to the image of the wandering of the spirit, which it symbolizes. In the search of the Chinese spirit for another life, another way and place in which to continue, it was discovered that this other life was accessible only under conditions discarded as irresponsible by the Chinese spirit, and that the spirit, if it wishes to continue, has to be content with this life.

In the search for a guide in this life, we find in this period of Chinese intellectual history a renewed trend toward the Book of Changes. The tradition of the book was actually never interrupted. But in agreement with the style of the period, the *I ching* research had concerned itself with imaginings and imaginations. These imaginings as such travel a course whose exploration is certainly justified. Thus an apocryphal literature on the Book of Changes

19. They pull the suncarriage.

20. The pheasant is transformed into a snake when it delves into the Huai River; the sparrow becomes a clam when it delves into the sea.

21. Another translation is in Zach, *Die chinesische Anthologie*, p. 329.

was produced at this time. Generally speaking, the apocrypha concern themselves with the static aspects of the book, with well-established landscapes of the spirit and circles of ideas. The focus of interest strayed from the dynamics of the book.

In the late third and in the fourth century, the life style of the period changed, in poetry as well as in *I ching* research, and we find a new interest in the concept of Change itself, toward the essence of this concept and toward the essence of the images contained in the book. It was rediscovered thereby that everything static, all established institutions and constructions, indeed everything patterned, were only the framework in which the Changes move. It is a frame, however, into which one must, as a rule, coordinate oneself, but which occasionally it is wise to escape.

The Book of Changes knows a number of constellations in which the frame of the established loses its meaning and in which the house of the father must be left behind. In all these cases the T'uan Commentary[22] points to the meaning of the time in which this happens. It appears here that the meaning of the time, then, was stronger than that which is represented by the framework of the established; the meaning of the dynamic impulse is stronger than tradition.

It must be pointed out that the word *meaning* (*Yi*) here refers to the given meaning (signification), and not the grasped meaning (significance); to the meaning one ascribes to a time situation and not the meaning one analyzes out of a time situation.[23] One's own judgment gives meaning to time in this case, and meaning is not something recognized in the situation as such. Therefore whoever finds himself in such a situation is not bound by a meaning inherent in the situation; he is called upon to make something meaningful out of the situation by his own judgment. It is with this under-

22. The Commentary on the Decision in the Wilhelm-Baynes translation.
23. See *Eranos Jahrbuch 1956* 26 (1957) :351–86, pp. 84–88, above.

standing of the word *meaning* that the T'uan Commentary says, in the mentioned cases, "The meaning of such a time is truly great." One of the hexagrams in which this is expressed is the fifty-sixth, *Lü*, The Wanderer.

Even apart from this hexagram, the idea of wandering is quite common in the Book of Changes. At different times we find expressed that the seasons wander and that sun and moon wander. Even more often than with such patterned movements, the world is used for motion of an unrestrained kind. Thus, it is said the clouds wander, the wind wanders, the water wanders, and the rolling of thunder wanders. And in the T'uan Commentary to Hexagram 2, *K'un*, The Receptive, it says that the mare, symbolic animal of the receptive, wanders the earth without bounds, with this added remark: "Thus the superior man has a direction in his wanderings."[24]

This sentence dips into the semantics of the word that stands for wandering (*hsing*). Wandering is taken here as simply going, putting one foot before the other one. It is not to let oneself go, but rather a treading of the way that leaves tracks on the path already walked. It is a movement with direction, a going that acquires a meaning. The active, significant element of this movement is so strong that the same word is used for action, carrying out.

Applied to human fate, our book points to several attributes of this situation. Wandering leads away from a given secure condition out into the unknown, and this unknown can assuredly be something dangerous. At six in the fifth place of Hexagram 51, *Chen*, The Arousing (Shock, Thunder), "one wanders in danger" through which one wanders, without losing anything at all.[25]

In nine at the beginning of Hexagram 36, *Ming*, Darkening of

24. Cf. Wilhelm-Baynes, p. 387.
25. Cf. ibid., p. 650.

the Light, the superior man, overcome by the "Darkening of the Light," finds nothing to eat for three days on his wanderings.[26] In nine in the third place of Hexagram 43, *Kuai*, Break-through, the superior man wanders lonely in the rain. He is bespattered and people murmur against him. But no blame is attached to these difficulties.[27]

The loneliness of wandering is mentioned several times. In six at the beginning of Hexagram 35, *Chin*, Progress, the one who progresses is suddenly turned back, to which the Image Commentary[28] remarks: "To wander alone is appropriate."[29]

However, the absence of company does not appear to be necessary in all cases. The six in the third place of Hexagram 41, *Sun*, The Decrease, has this text: "When three people journey together, their number decreases by one. When one man journeys alone, he finds a companion."[30]

The wandering together of two seems only possible when they are both of one mind, when, as the Great Treatise says at this place, "the effect of becoming one" commences.[31] Otherwise, the problem of leadership arises. In the situation of wandering, to be led is indicated only in exceptional cases, and even where it might be indicated, it is usually refused. Twice this is expressed in the same words. The nine in the fourth place of the forty-third hexagram, The Break-through, which possibly points to the works of the great Yü, has this text: "There is no skin on his thighs and walking comes hard. If a man were to let himself be led like a sheep, remorse would disappear. But if these words are heard, they would not be believed."[32]

26. Ibid., p. 566.
27. Ibid., p. 605.
28. The b commentary of ibid.
29. Cf. ibid., p. 561.
30. Ibid., p. 592.
31. Ibid., p. 593.
32. Ibid., p. 606.

The nine in the third place of Hexagram 44, *Kou*, Coming to Meet, says: "There is no skin on his thighs and walking comes hard. If one is mindful of the danger, no great mistake is made. The Image Commentary remarks on that: "He still walks, without being led."[33]

Wandering, then, leads out of the entanglements of given laws into a freedom in which the rules of tradition no longer prevail. The book at one point expresses this in a very humorous way. In six in the third place of Hexagram 25, *Wu Wang*, Innocence (The Unexpected), a situation is pictured in which the wanderer filches a cow that a citizen had tied up. The text comments solely: "The wanderer's gain is the citizen's loss."[34]

The figure of the wanderer was not an unusual sight in society during Chou times. There were the journeying knights, as with us, who had taken it upon themselves to fight injustice and oppression on their own. There were the prophets and scholars whose mission it was to spread news and knowledge. Usually the roads were open and hospitality certain. The Image text for Hexagram 24, *Fu*, Turning Point, remarks, however, that during the time of the solstice, the passes were closed and wanderers and merchants were not traveling.[35]

The figure of the wanderer that appears in this text is designated by the word *lü*. This is also the word used as the name of the fifty-sixth hexagram. The semantics of this word come from a specific aspect of wandering, originally representing soldiers on the march. Even today the same word is used for a division, as a military unit. But it has always had the meaning "to wander" at least since the early age of Chou, and in the modern word for "wandering" or "traveling," *lü-hsing*, it has been united with the above-mentioned word *hsing*.

33. Ibid., p. 611.
34. Cf. ibid., p. 512.
35. Cf. ibid., p. 506.

The original meaning of the word may help achieve an understanding of how the Book of Changes interprets the situation of the wanderer. We find here that wandering is considered mandatory, a fate determined by military command, not a voluntary leaving home in search of another life. It is travel determined by fate, and even when, as is the case in the texts of the fifty-sixth hexagram, the power determining this fate is no longer the military command, but rather a constellation of an entirely different kind, it still leads to homelessness and danger. To give such a time situation meaning and to act meaningfully in it are the problems posed by the fifty-sixth hexagram.

The mentioned characteristics of the situation of wandering are inexorably laid down in our hexagram. The book *Tsa-Kua* (Miscellaneous Notes) says: "He who has few friends, this is the wanderer."[36]

And the book *Hsü-Kua* (The Sequence) says:

> Whatever greatness [referring to the hexagram *Feng*] may exhaust itself upon, this much is certain, it loses its home. Hence there follows the hexagram The Wanderer. The wanderer has nothing that might receive him.

And yet, stared at by this fate, the T'uan Commentary says: "The meaning of the time of the wanderer is truly great."

In the Book of Changes the sign *Lü* follows the sign *Feng* (Abundance), of which it is the obverse.

Another opposite to the sign *Lü* is Hexagram 60, *Chieh*, Limitation:

36. For quotes from the 56th hexagram see ibid., pp. 674–79.

It may be abundance or limitation, therefore, that will bring about the fate of the wanderer.

The constellation of the trigrams of the fifty-sixth hexagram shows the sign of *Li*, The Clinging, above the sign *Ken*, Keeping Still. The basis here is therefore the mountain, but also the pass over the mountain, which leads to other landscapes beyond the watershed, and the mountain path, stony and steep, upon which alone one can reach these landscapes. It is the sign in which God brings creatures to perfection.[37] The attribute Keeping Still is weighty, however, and in the first place is meant as a holding-still-for-fate. Over it stands the sign for fire, the sun, light, and clarity, the sign in which God causes creatures to perceive one another, the sign of recognition of the previously unknown, the sign of the seeing eye, the sign of the consuming fire but also of lightning, and the sign of defensive and offensive weapons.

Here, too, the attribute of clinging dependence, again on fate, which is given in the image of the mountain, appears decisive. The fire on the mountain may blaze like a beacon, but its direction-giving light is dependent upon products of the mountain. The image of the fire on the mountain reminds one of the agricultural occupations of early China where, under the usages of slash and burn economy, groups of farmers left the safety of the walled town in springtime and moved to the mountains, to burn off brush and woods, in order to make room for food production. Such movement from safety into the wilderness was accompanied by certain licenses, and so the Image Commentary says: "Fire on the mountain: the image of the wanderer. Thus the superior man is clear minded and cautious in imposing penalties and protracts no lawsuits."

37. Ibid., p. 268.

The T'uan Commentary then no longer refers to the wandering farmer groups, but to the fate of the individual wanderer: "Keeping still and adhering to clarity; hence success in small things."

From the Image it also takes the guiding principle that the subjection to fate of the wanderer may not deteriorate into a self-abandonment. The central line of the upper trigram is soft and yielding, but is flanked by two strong lines. The situation of the wanderer is uncertainty, danger, and homelessness, and he does well to take this situation into account. His mission is to give such a situation meaning and to find a goal in it; he must persist with this mission even when insight into its meaning arrives only gradually. The T'uan Commentary derives this from the Judgment text, which says: "Success through smallness (or in small ways). Perseverance brings good fortune to the wanderer."

The line texts that describe the way stations of the wanderer point to danger right from the start. The six at the beginning says: "The wanderer busies himself with trivial things. In this way he draws misfortune upon himself."

The described situation becomes clearer by referring to the opposite of this line, the nine at the beginning of Hexagram 30, *Li*, The Clinging Fire, where the text reads: "The footprints run crisscross. If one is seriously [reverentially] intent [concentrating on one's goal], no blame."

The path to be chosen is not given yet, one is still experimenting and runs crisscross. These difficulties at the beginning as such are not harmful if one does not forget the goal because of them. The wanderer at his first station is exactly in this danger. The Small Image Commentary says: "His will is spent [he loses his goal] and this is a misfortune."[38]

The second station brings his first rest. The text says: "The wanderer comes to an inn. He carries his property with him [ver-

38. Ibid., p. 537.

[182]

batim: in his bosom].³⁹ He wins the steadfastness of a young servant."

Here the wanderer has become fully conscious of his fate and also of what he has to offer, in view of his fate. He comes to the inn and achieves a temporary resting place and a generous, even a jealousy-arousing meal.⁴⁰ What is more, he wins the above-mentioned companion in his wandering (again temporary) in the person of the young servant, and the problem of leadership appears in the relationship immediately. For the moment, however, he may leave all inherent problems out of consideration.

Such rest during a journey is not permanent. Thus the text of nine in the third place says: "The wanderer burns down his inn.⁴¹ He loses the steadfastness of his young servant. Danger."

The strong line here acknowledges the given danger and knows that further progress is necessary. The wanderer sharply separates himself from everything that could lead to permanent ties and new entanglements. The resting place is burned, even though that is a loss for him, as the Little Image Commentary remarks, and leads him into danger. He also has to separate himself from his companion since human relationships of this kind have no place during a journey. The Image Commentary says here: "As a wanderer to deal with a subordinate: it is right to lose him."⁴²

Only by this incisive cut does it become possible to step into the upper trigram, which alone can produce clarity for him. As in many other cases, the first line of the upper trigram leads to doubts, even to despondence. The text of the nine in the third place says, "The wanderer rests in a shelter. He obtains his property and an ax. My heart is not glad."

39. Cf. *Omnia mea mecum porto.*
40. See Hex. 50, 9/2, Wilhelm-Baynes, p. 644.
41. I depart here slightly from my father's translation.
42. Again I depart somewhat from my father's translation.

This transition thus produces a further pause. What the situation offers here is not, as in the second line, an inn with its convenience, but only a place where one can stay, without finding a harbor. "He does not obtain a position,"[43] the Little Image Commentary explains. Nevertheless several losses, brought about by the blaze in the aforementioned line, can be compensated for: The wanderer gets his property back. The value of this property has fallen, to be sure, after the experiences he lived through. It is necessary for what is to come, but taken by itself, is not sufficient as a basis for self-confidence and confidence in his own fate.

Further, the wanderer gets an ax, a tool necessary for the continuation of his dangerous journey. And so the text adds a verse similar to one occasionally used in stanzas of the Book of Songs: "My heart is not glad."

This interlude serves as a time of self-contemplation, the keeping still of the rump and meditative exercises by which one forgets the ego and is led beyond it.[44] Leading back to the self and its transpersonal aspects makes the ego relative and permits personal fate to lose its weight, even though its impetus still persists.

Armed thus, the wanderer reaches the high point of his journey. The text of the six in the fifth place says: "He shoots a pheasant. It drops with the first arrow. In the end comes an honorable commission."[45]

43. Literally "not yet." The "yet" is, however, a phrasing of the commentary whose Confucianistically tainted expectations the further lines of the hexagram will not fulfill.

44. This is indicated by the 6/4 of the 52nd hexagram (Wilhelm-Baynes, p. 203) that is arrived at when this line changes. The interplay of trigrams in Hex. 56 is particularly intimate. When the lower line of the upper trigram changes the result is Hex. 52, which is a doubling of the lower trigram. When the lower line of the lower trigram changes, the result is Hex. 30, which is a doubling of the upper trigram. Just as in the first line anticipation of light and fire comes into play, here we have a persistence of "keeping still," an attitude that one believed to have already transcended.

45. Again I depart somewhat from my father's translation.

The pheasant is the animal symbol of the upper trigram *Li*. This bird was considered one of the great delicacies of the Chinese kitchen. As such it was often used as an introductory gift to the rulers of the age. As a sign of the impersonalization of fate, the essence of clarity is sacrificed and brought as a tribute. This action is so proper that the problem of success is no longer of importance. In this situation it is obvious that the pheasant is downed with the first arrow; it is obvious that it will be accepted by rulers as the gift of a guest; it is obvious that the "property" of the wanderer, his intellectual gifts, their value made relative in the meantime, would impress the ruler, and it is obvious that an honorable commission follows.

The problem of the line is that the wanderer does not lose his wanderer's nature. He may and must sacrifice everything personal; he may honorably carry out a time-determined commission, but even under such set personal conditions he may not pursue a permanent position and a lasting field of endeavor. After fulfilling his commission he is ordained to retreat, friendly and without bitterness, but he may not remain.[46]

The alternative to this retreat is described in the upper nine, where the text reads: "The bird burns his nest. The wanderer laughs at first then he must need lament and weep. He loses his cow in I.[47] Misfortune."

As so often with the upper line of a hexagram, the security within (and constraints of) one's own fate, which already appeared relative in the line before it, is completely lost. The wanderer, who has divorced himself from his fate here, must live through the experience that his fate withdraws completely from his guidance, fulfills itself in independent ways, and thereby thrusts the wanderer into final misfortune. The bird here burns his nest. This conflicting

46. See Hex. 33, 9/5, Wilhelm-Baynes, p. 132.
47. On this reading see *Eranos Jahrbuch 1956* 36 (1957):358–59; p. 59, above.

situation is expressed in six at the top of Hexagram 62, *Hsiao Kuo*, Preponderance of the Small, which is reached when our line changes. There he goes past his fate full of conceit and does not meet it, whereupon the flying bird leaves him.[48] The burning of the nest reminds one of the phoenix archetype. In the earliest Chou era, the phoenix was not yet known. It was not until later that it became so richly endowed with mythology in China. Several of its archetypal characteristics were connected with the pheasant in those days. The burning of the nest reminds one of the conflagration of the Twilight of the Gods, which ends the fate of the wanderer in Western mythology.

In our line the wanderer at this time believes he is allowed to enjoy an apparent freedom from fate, and breaks out into uncontrolled merriment. Soon it is demonstrated to him that in his irresponsibility he has lost his essence. The cow, symbol of the receptive, the connection with the earth, is taken from him, and his laughter changes to bitter lament. It is an inexorable solution, to which the Little Image Commentary adds: "As a wanderer to be haughty: the burning is valid. He loses his cow in I: he finally would not hear."

In order to coordinate the picture of the wanderer, whose contours we have delineated here, with the theme of this lecture, the wandering of the spirit, we must look at still another hexagram, the twentieth, *Kuan*, Contemplation (View):

In this hexagram the lines of the bottom trigram of the wanderer hexagram

appear doubled. The Chinese word that gave the twentieth hexagram its name is derived from a pair of scales. The view here is

48. See Wilhelm-Baynes, p. 243.

not the individualizing impression of the senses, but a measured seeing, an overview that sees and weighs things in their relationships, that is, a contemplating view. The word, as so often in Chinese, means both the viewing and viewed image. This is expressed in *Tsa-kua* (Miscellaneous Notes), where it says: "The view is giving [the viewed image] and taking [the viewing]."[49]

The complex of lines of Hexagram 20, *Kuan*, Contemplation, is a very high mountain, a viewpoint permitting a wide view and also a spiritual observation. The constellation of the trigrams "wind over earth" offers possibly another perspective on this insight, which ties together the twentieth hexagram with the Wanderer hexagram. The Image Commentary expresses it thus: "The wind blows over the earth: the image of contemplation. So the old kings visited the regions of the world, contemplated the people, and gave them instruction."

The attitude in which this contemplation is carried out is clothed by the Judgment text in a superbly strong picture: "The ablution has been made but not yet the offering. Full of trust [in expectation of truth] they look up to him."

Contemplation is placed here at the moment of greatest tension right before the offering of the great sacrifice, when all preparations had been completed. Contained in this moment is an expectation. For those who are supposed to be consecrated by the sacrifice, this expresses itself in highest trust, and for the one who carries out the sacrifice, in the highest consciousness of the sacramental function of this deed. This anticipatory expectation is the attitude in which the contemplation is consummated.

From the steps of contemplation the beginning six speaks of boylike contemplation, of unself-conscious, unreflective looking, therefore, that sees things just as they are and not yet in their relationship. Experience, which offers relationships, is not yet pres-

49. For quotes from the 20th hexagram see ibid., pp. 485–89.

[187]

ent. But this is the beginning, and experience can only be acquired in this way.

The six in the second place brings contemplation through the crack in the door, and adds to it: "The perseverance of a woman furthers." One can naturally see through a crack in the door in two directions. One can look out and have an early, if limited view of the relationships of the world. Because of its limitations, the concept of the world will naturally be subjective. But one can also look inside through the crack in the door into one's self and through the self into the mysterious relationships of life. For both directions of view the woman is the one called upon here.

The six in the third place has the text: "Contemplation of my life: advance or retreat?"

This is definitely the looking inside, the introverted contemplation, the weighing of one's worth, and relative to that, the weighing of one's own position. Images that determine one's future are taken from this introverted contemplation. It produces images that determine the direction of action, advance or retreat.

The text of six in the fourth place reads: "Contemplation of the splendor of the kingdom. It furthers one to dwell as the guest of a king."

Here the view goes out and sees the splendor of the great relationships. On the basis of this view one arrives at a position that corresponds to that of six of the fifth place of the Wanderer hexagram. One dwells as the guest of a ruler, whose business requires such a view. Notice that one is still a guest, and not in a permanent position. Only in this way can the view be converted, unhindered by bureaucratic considerations, into effective work—in the highest commission.[50]

The high point of the hexagram then leads again to an inner view. The text reads simply: "Contemplation of my life."

One contemplates oneself and meets oneself again in the arche-

50. See Hex. 12, 9/4, ibid., p. 54.

type of the school of fishes, and thereby becomes integrated again into the onerous business of living.[51]

Even the upper line, the one retired from and transcending the world, occupies itself with life. The text says here: "Contemplation of life."

This is the view outward, from a high lookout, upon life down here.

This view of the spirit, the view inside as well as the world view, offers images taken not from speculative but from practical life. The hexagram points singlemindedly to life itself.

We find this word again in a definition of the concept of Change in the Great Treatise: "Change is gushing life,"[52] verbatim: life-giving life; the procreating of procreation; the begetting of birth. And this calls to memory a much-cited passage from the Great Treatise: "The greatest virtue between heaven and earth is to live."[53]

51. See Hex. 23, 6/5, ibid., p. 96. The Little Image Commentary interprets this self-contemplation as a reflected one. It says: "Contemplation of my life, that is contemplation of the people." This can be understood and has been understood as a contemplation of the effects of one's own life. It can, however, also be understood as meeting oneself again within the great stream of the people.

52. Ibid., p. 299.

53. Cf. ibid., p. 328.

VII

THE INTERPLAY OF
IMAGE AND CONCEPT

Among the fragments of creation myths that are preserved in the Chinese tradition, there are some that can be pieced together into a mythological unit that has been termed the Myth of the Cosmogonic Egg.[1] In it the primordial stage of creation is perceived as an undifferentiated mass, the Chaos (Chinese, *Hun-tun*). Reports on this Chaos differ. In some it is the stage from which creation proceeded, in others it is in itself the product of the first act of creation, that is to say, it is put in the same place as the *tohu-wa-bohu* stage of the biblical creation story. The reports generally agree, however, in describing the shape of the Chaos as something spherical. At times it is described as something like a bag, or a sack; at times, with certain color patterns on its surface; at times, even with six legs and two batlike wings that make it capable of

1. For this and the following see: Wolfram Eberhard, *Lokalkulturen im alten China* II (Peking: Catholic University, 1942), pp. 467–77 and passim; Kwang-chih Chang, "The Chinese Creation Myths: A Study in Method," *Bulletin of the Institute of Ethnology*, Academia Sinica, no. 8 (Autumn 1959), pp. 47–79 (Chinese with English abstract). Mircea Eliade has dealt with the world-wide distribution of this phenomenon in his *Patterns in Comparative Religion* (Cleveland: Meridian Books, 1963), pp. 413–16.

locomotion, but without any openings, particularly without ears and eyes. Mockingly the book *Chuang-tzu* refers to this creature as playing the host to the Great Kings of the Southern and the Northern Sea who then, out of gratitude, wanted to bore holes into the Chaos so that it may see, hear, eat, and breathe, but when they had finished boring the holes, the Chaos had died.[2] Most frequently the Chaos is perceived in the shape of an egg out of which, through some development or creative act, the world differentiated. This motif has even entered the myth of P'an-Ku,[3] who is said to have lived within the egg, growing there every day and thereby prying heaven and earth apart. The separation of heaven and earth out of the cosmogonic egg is almost uniformly the first act of this process of creation.

Chinese philosophy has then developed this world egg myth into the yin-yang concept, a concept that is, of course, eminently pertinent to the topic of this year's meeting, the polarity of life. This development was consummated within a school of natural scientists whose main representative is Tsou Yen. Unfortunately all the major writings of this school have been lost. Reflections about their social status and some of their ideas survive, however, and from this it emerges that they must have been the most advanced group of thinkers during the fourth and third centuries B.C. The rulers of the time vied with each other for their services, and Needham has, I believe justifiably, compared their attractiveness to that of the atomic scientists in the forties of our century.[4] As far as we can see, the yin-yang concept developed by this school has never been separated completely from the world egg myth. As a later compendium states bluntly: "[In the beginning], heaven

2. See *Chuangtzu* 7.7; see Burton Watson, *The Complete Works of Chuang Tzu* (New York: Columbia University Press, 1968), p. 97.

3. On which see pp. 29–30, above.

4. Joseph Needham, *Science and Civilisation in China* (Cambridge: At the University Press, 1954–), 2:232 et seq.

and earth were in the state of chaos [*hun-tun*], which was shaped like an egg. . . . After 18,000 years heaven and earth split apart, the yang, being limpid, formed heaven, the yin, being turbid, formed earth."

What confronts us in a statement like this is, in addition to the polarity between yin and yang, a polarity of a different order, the polarity between two layers of the human mind. On the one hand the evocative power of archetypal imagery is not discarded but apprehended and expressed in appropriate linguistic and narrative forms, and on the other, we find the discursive power of human reasoning. Image and concept confront each other here, not as hostile twins but in an intricate interplay, supporting and elucidating each other in different ways in order to clarify the polarities of the phenomenal world and of human life taking place in this world, inasmuch as this world is a product and a replica of the polarity within the human mind.

In the later layers of the Book of Changes, the so-called Ten Wings, language deriving from the yin-yang concept is abundantly applied. Because the original writings of the yin-yang school have all been lost, the Ten Wings are our best source of information about the concerns of this school. It should be kept in mind, though, that a new concept was put to work here in a very old context. It is thus quite difficult, if not impossible, to determine which attributes and characteristics of the yin-yang concept merged into the Book of Changes and which accrued to the yin-yang concept from the older tradition of the Book. It will be stressed, as we go along, that the old tradition of the *I ching* also worked with concepts as well as with images. It would thus be a fallacy to argue that whatever discursive reasoning occurs in the later layers might be considered a contribution of the yin-yang school. This would, however, not exclude the assumption that the conceptual aspect of the Book has been strengthened, sharpened, and to a degree elucidated by an application of the conceptual tools of this school.

To begin with, the yin and the yang have been identified with, or at least coordinated to, the divided and the undivided lines that make up the structure of the hexagrams. They have furthermore been identified with or coordinated to the trigrams (not the hexagrams) *K'un*, The Receptive, and *Ch'ien*, The Creative; and they have finally been coordinated with those other trigrams in which the divided or the undivided line is dominant, that is to say, *Sun*, *Li*, and *Tui* for yin and *Chen*, *K'an* and *Ken* for yang.

These coordinations are of interest in at least two respects. They do, on the one hand, help to clarify what the yin and the yang concept represent. It is alluring to assume that by coordination with the trigrams *K'un* and *Ch'ien* whatever these trigrams stand for would implicitly be carried also by the yin and the yang. There is a pre-Confucian lore, enumerating phenomena and ideas belonging to the individual trigrams, which in a somewhat systematized form is found in the book *Shuo-kua* (Discussion of the Trigrams). It appears, however, that the abundance of these attributes has been rather conscientiously avoided when the Wings talk about the yin and the yang. Their attributes as specifically stated in the Wings add to their original meaning darkness and light, devotion for yin and strength for yang, yielding to the extent of weakness for yin and firmness to the extent of rigidity for yang. They are made there to represent the cosmic entities of earth and heaven, the moon and the sun, and the social entities of the little man and the gentleman. In political life yin represents the official and yang the ruler, in family life, yin the wife and yang the husband. Strangely, a number of characteristics for the yin are mentioned to which the correspondences for the yang are not stated. The *Wen-yen* commentary to the lines of the *K'un* hexagram makes a more extensive use of the yin concept than the corresponding commentary of the *Ch'ien* hexagram. It is stated there that the yin might congeal and that, even though it possesses beauty, it has the tendency to veil it. No more than a guess is possible as to which of these associations were contributions of the yin-yang concept and which came from the original lore of the Book of Changes.[5]

A second point of interest that emerges from the way in which the yin-yang concept is treated in the Ten Wings concerns the particular positions in which and from which this concept is made to work. No dialectical formula has been preserved, if ever one existed, dealing with the way in which this concept operates. From the field of operation, however, to which this concept was applied, it can be deduced that it did not constitute an overriding dialectical principle. To be sure, the yin and the yang as a rule worked in relationship to each other, but they always worked within and from a given position. As has been mentioned, within the structure of the Book of Changes the units of identification of the yin and the yang were the individual lines and the trigrams but not the hexagrams. This means that the yin-yang concept works within the structure of the hexagrams and within the system of the Book but does not determine one or the other.

This limited application leaves a wide and complex field of operation for the yin and the yang. Afer all, each position within the hexagram, from the lowliest to the most exalted, can be occupied by either a yin or a yang, and each position, whether occupied by a yin or a yang, stands in a given relationship to each other position, which in turn can be occupied by a yin or a yang. If we add to this the main insight of the Book, to which again the yin-yang concept gives powerful expression, that ours is a world of change and that no position or relationship is forever static, the many-faceted complexity of the field of operation of the yin and yang becomes apparent.

And then, the actual or potential relationship between the yin

5. These attributes of the yin and the yang are given in the *Wen-yen* commentaries to the first two hexagrams and in occasional remarks in the Great Treatise and the Little Images.

and the yang is not only determined by their intrinsic qualities but also by their relative positions. A ruler will certainly relate differently to an official depending on whether his position is above or below this official. There are, of course, optimum relative positions from which the mutual interaction of the yin and the yang is bound to work harmoniously. But such ideal situations are rarely achieved. In the majority of cases the degree of harmony and antagonism between the yin and the yang has to be worked out within the context of the, to be sure, temporary positions they occupy at a given moment of time. Whenever the situation allows a joining of the powers of the yin and the yang, the potential of the situation will receive form, as the Great Treatise puts it.[6] At the extreme opposite, however, the situation will fail of solution and even battle might ensue.

This is argued in terms of trigrams in the T'uan Commentaries of Hexagrams 11 and 12, *T'ai* and *P'i*, Peace and Stagnation. These two hexagrams, as will be recalled, are composed of the trigrams *Ch'ien* and *K'un*, the prime examples among the trigrams of the yang and the yin. In the hexagram *T'ai*, the yang occupies the position below the yin; they are in a harmonious relationship from which the process of peace follows. In the *P'i* hexagram, where the yang assumes the outer and the yin the inner position, stagnation is the consequence.

A dramatic incident of a battle is described in the topmost line of the *K'un* hexagram occupied by a yin that under the prevailing circumstances can only be interpreted as an usurpation. Here the yin and yang dragon are locked in battle as a consequence of which both suffer. A corresponding situation is referred to in the book *Shuo-kua*. You will recall that beautiful passage in which the manifestations of the Lord on High within the cycle of trigrams are described. Here the Lord on High is said to battle in the sign of the

6. Wilhelm-Baynes, pp. 345–46.

[195]

Creative; in this situation, all yang, the dark and the light, arouse each other.[7]

The special qualities and attributes of the yin and the yang as well as the given positions within and from which they work determine, however, the limitations of this concept. This might have been only dimly understood during the period of high rationality in which this concept found its way into the Book of Changes. There is, however, one passage in the Great Treatise that speaks of aspects that cannot be fathomed (*ts'e*, to plumb the depths of) in terms of yin and yang. These aspects are called *shen*, which my father translates as spirit.[8] The yin-yang concept, a polarized system designed to work within the world of phenomena, will, with all its usefulness, of necessity leave unexamined many of the concerns of the Book of Changes. For an understanding of these we might proceed to apply a different kind of polarity that is found within and not outside of the human mind.

The later layers of the Book of Changes, particularly the Great Treatise, deal in occasional remarks with the question of how knowledge and understanding are arrived at. There appears to have been some insight into the epistemological problem involved here; witness the following conversation, which is supposed to have taken place between Confucius and his disciples:

The Master said: "Writing cannot express words exhaustively, words cannot express ideas exhaustively."

This is followed by the dismayed question: "Then one cannot see the ideas of the Saints and Sages?"

Whereupon the Master answers: "The Saints and Sages established images in order to express their ideas exhaustively."[9]

In this conversation apprehension and comprehension are traced back to the images as their sole source. The pertinence of this

7. Ibid., pp. 268–70.
8. Ibid., p. 301.
9. Cf. ibid., p. 322.

[196]

insight to the concerns of our Book is expressed strongly. As one remark has it. "The Changes consist of images."[10] Or, in another passage: "The eight trigrams speak [or: proclaim] through their images." Also the function of these images is expressed strongly: "The Changes contain images in order to reveal," we read here, or: "Through the service of the images things are comprehended." What these images are, how they can be apprehended and "established," and how they can lead to comprehension is then dealt with in a number of other passages.

The most elementary answer to the first question is formulated thus: "What appears is called an image." This "what appears," or more succinctly "what appears to the eye," is offered by the universe, by heaven and earth. The appearances thus offered include heaven and earth themselves, which are called "the greatest model images." In the already somewhat systematized thinking of the Great Treatise, a distinction is made between what heaven and what earth offers. Primordial images are offered by heaven. It is repeatedly said that they hang down from heaven or that heaven dangles them down. Earth offers forms or shapes (*hsing*) or even institutions (*fa*): "In heaven primal images take form, on earth shapes take form. This is the way change and transformation are revealed."[11]

In order to establish these images they will then have to be represented. Talking about established images, the Great Treatise very frequently says: "Images are representations." This process of representation is accomplished in the verbiage of the Book by "the Saints and Sages" who, like great artisans or artists, work from celestial images and mundane shapes as their models. The process does involve a creative act. At one point the Great Treatise says directly: "The establishment of images is called creative."

10. This and the following quotes are taken from different sections of the Great Treatise.
11. Cf. Wilhelm-Baynes, p. 280.

Like all creative processes, this representation involves a degree of abstraction that, according to circumstances, may be stronger or weaker and may at times remove the representation rather far from its model without losing its character as a representation. As an example, a rather extreme passage will be quoted here:

> [The words] good fortune and misfortune are representations of gain and loss; remorse and humiliation are representations of sorrow and forethought.
>
> Change and transformation are representations of progress and retrogression. The firm and the yielding are representations of day and night.[12]

Or, conversely, the essay on cultural history in the Great Treatise may be referred to here in which cultural implements and institutions are explained as representations of images presented by certain ones among the hexagrams.

This creative representation has, however, to be preceded by an apprehension of the images. The Great Treatise has paid much attention to the mental process involved here and has discoursed on it in a number of beautifully formulated passages. Thus, the introduction to the essay on cultural history referred to a moment ago reads:

> When in early antiquity Pao Hsi ruled the world, he looked upward and contemplated the images in the heavens; he looked downward and contemplated the patterns on earth. He contemplated the markings of birds and beasts and their adaptations to the regions. He proceeded directly from himself and indirectly from the objects. Thus he invented the eight trigrams in order to enter into connection with the virtues of the light of the gods and to regulate the conditions of all beings.[13]

It is thus not simple recognition but the process of contemplation through which the contact between the self and the images is

12. Ibid., pp. 288–89.
13. Cf. ibid., pp. 328–29.

consummated. In another passage we read: "The Saints and Sages were able to survey all the confused diversities under heaven. They contemplated forms and phenomena and made representations of things and their attributes. These were called the Images."[14]

The term *contemplation* already figures prominently in the older layers of the Book of Changes. An entire hexagram is devoted to it there in which different ways of contemplating and different objects of contemplation are discussed.

Once the images are established through contemplation, or even independently of this creative act, another mental process comes into play. The passage continues:

> The Saints and Sages were able to survey all the movements under heaven. They contemplated the way in which these movements met and became interrelated, to take their course according to eternal laws. Then they appended judgments, to distinguish between the good fortune and misfortune indicated. These were called the Judgments.[15]

This mental act of exercising judgment, leading to pronounced judgments, brings about another type of insight, an insight into what is called here the meeting and interrelationship of movements and their eternal laws. In other words, it is a conceptual insight that is observed here, a quest for the concept as a related opposite to the image. The human mind, contemplating and passing judgments, thus establishes the polarity between image and concept.

When we now proceed to apply these speculations based on the later layers of the Book of Changes to its earlier texts, it will become apparent that the interrelatedness of image and concept was at that time still quite intimate. It is not possible to identify among the older texts those that talk either purely in images or purely in concepts, even though, in a very general way, it can be said that the line texts, particularly in their assumed earliest versions, deal

14. Cf. ibid., p. 304.
15. Cf. ibid.

mainly in images and the Judgment texts predominantly in concepts. There are instances of hexagrams in whose texts this distinction is entirely true, such as the very first one in which the Judgment text talks about sublimity, potentiality of success, power to further, and perseverance, that is to say, concepts throughout, whereas the line texts show the different stages of the dragon's progress. In other instances no such neat distinction can be made. Thus, the Judgment text of the ninth hexagram, The Taming Power of the Small, adds to the concept "success" the image: "Dense clouds, no rain from our western region."[16] In a very general way it can, however, be said that the Judgment texts are more inclined to issue concepts, whereas the line texts contemplate and represent images.

Another depository for concepts are the names of the hexagrams. Many of these are, of course, pure images, such as The Caldron, The Marrying Maiden, Biting Through, and others. Many others are, however, undoubtedly concepts, such as Innocence, Progress and Retreat, Influence, Modesty, and others. It is an interesting phenomenon that many of these conceptual names of hexagrams are so-called *hapax legomena;* they do not occur in the earlier literature at places other than these names, and a number of them have never even been used in the later literature except in passages directly derivative from these hexagrams. What we observe here is apparently an attempt to create and formulate concepts for specific purposes, if not to define them. We stand witness here to the first manifestation of a new stage in the self-realization of the human mind in which the faculty of judgment is first exercised and leads to abstractions distinct from images. In a number of cases the derivation of these newly established concepts from given images is fairly obvious, such as the concept of conduct from the image of treading on something (just like in the German *Auftreten*). It would be a fallacy, however, to reduce these concepts entirely to

16. Ibid., p. 40.

their image antecedents and to deny to the authors of these early texts the faculty of abstraction that is reflected in these terms. It is a different mental faculty, newly awakened, than the one that contemplates and represents images. A realization of this faculty only renders to the hexagrams their tension, their clarity, and their authority. As we go along, this, I hope, will be clarified in a number of individual instances.

Returning to the images, it might be worth contemplating for a while the sources from which the images of the earlier texts are taken. To establish collectively valid images, we in the West have gotten accustomed to consult and contemplate a number of specific sources: dreams, let us say, or mythology, religious traditions and performances, and possibly the works of creative artists. Most, but not all of these sources are also known to the authors of the Book of Changes. For reasons that are obvious and do not have to be gone into here, the works of creative artists do not occur in the earlier texts, and also dreams are never specifically mentioned. There are, however, situations in the Book that appear like perfect dream images. The meeting syndrome might serve as an example here. The image of meeting, that is to say fated encounter, occurs in three different hexagrams. It occurs to begin with, in Hexagram 38, K'uei, Opposition, a constellation in which the polarity is determined by a lack of affinity of the two poles to each other brought about by specific given circumstances. It is the opposition of the second and the youngest daughter, the mailed heroine and the sorceress. But also these opposed poles are fated to meet. Thus one meets his lord in a narrow alley in the situation of the nine in the second place, the position in which action, or at least preparations for action start. A narrow alley is an entirely unexpected place of encounter with one's lord. And in the nine in the fourth place one meets, when isolated through opposition, quite dangerously, his original master or fellow with whom even association occurs. Both these encounters have very much the quality of dream fates through which the polarity might be resolved and thus, again entirely unexpectedly, in a situation in which unpropitious aspects abound, one meets at the last moment the blessing of rain. A meeting with one's lord is then referred to in Hexagram 55, *Feng*, Abundance, a peak situation that is of necessity of short duration. Here one meets at the nine at the beginning his destined ruler who is recognized as such not due to previous experience, but through that immediate certainty that only a dream provides, and in spite of the fatefulness of this encounter, the association with him is only short. Similarly one meets at the nine in the fourth place in a situation of artificial darkness, brought about by unnatural circumstances, the ruler who is of like kind, an encounter in which the mutual affinity is recognized due to the guidance of the polestars whose light is revealed in the prevailing darkness. Such dream-destined encounters are then finally referred to in Hexagram 62, *Hsiao Kuo*, Preponderance of the Small. Here at the six in the second place one is out to meet the ancestor, passes him by, and meets the ancestress instead; or one is out to meet his prince but cannot reach him and meets the official instead. At the nine in the fourth place the encounter is not passed by but is actually consummated, a situation that again unexpectedly does not lead to rejoicing or fulfillment, but calls for utter caution and restraint. And finally, nightmarishly dreamlike, there is the six in the sixth place where one passes him by, not meeting him, a situation that, somewhat redundantly, is explained as bad luck and injury.

So much for images that might possibly have been taken from dream situations. Images coming from the religious tradition and from religious observances are used frequently in the Book of Changes, particularly the sacrifices and stations within the great sacrificial drama. I have dealt with these images in a different context.[17] Surprisingly, little use has been made in the Book of mytho-

17. In *Harvest* (Analytical Psychology Club of London), 1957; reprinted in *Spring 1972*, pp. 74–89.

logical imagery. This statement needs some qualification, though. It is quite possible that many more images could be traced back to mythological sources, if the mythological references had not been lost. It is quite possible, for instance, that the tied-up sack of the six in the fourth place of the second hexagram is a reference to the *Hun-tun* myth, the myth of the Chaos.[18] As things stand, we have to content ourselves with comparatively few references. The most obvious, and as a matter of fact the only entirely unquestionable mythological image in the Book, is the dragon, which occurs in the line texts of the first hexagram. Here we have, if we accept a reconstruction of the original version of these texts, something like a dragon ballad in which the dragon's progress is described in line after line: the dragon submerged in the subterranean waters, the dragon appearing above ground in the wet field, the dragon feeling dry in these shallow waters at the end of the day, leading to a creative resolve and the leap over the abyss, the dragon having conquered his new field of action, majestically flying in the heavens, and finally the exalted dragon.

Dragon lore is, of course, richly represented in later Chinese mythology. In it he appears with aspects and functions very similar to those of our Western dragons with the only exception, perhaps, that human behavior toward him is somewhat different: he is not being fed virgins and he is not being slain by St. Georges and Siegfrieds. There is no direct counterpart in mythological narrative to the dragon ballad of the first hexagram, but nonliterary evidence abounds to show that the dragon was one of the most prominent mythological figures of early China.[19]

The first hexagram may then serve here as the first example of the specific interplay between image and concept. The hexagram

18. See Marcel Granet, *Danses et légendes de la Chine ancienne* (Paris: F. Alcan, 1926), 2: 543.

19. Erwin Rousselle, "Drache und Stute," *Chinesisch-Deutscher Almanach* (1935), pp. 6–17.

bears the name The Creative, *Ch'ien*. Just as Eve out of the rib of Adam, this concept has been developed out of the image but has then, just like Eve, assumed a life of its own. The same is true, of course, for our Western term, which is based on the image of the creation of the world. The Chinese term *ch'ien* carries no such connotations. It is derived from the dragon image or, more precisely, from a particular phase of the dragon's progress. In the third line we have observed the dragon, after having spent a day in the shallow wet fields, prostrate from dryness, an apprehension that leads him to the creative resolve to conquer the heavens. Out of this apprehension the concept of the Creative has been developed. The Chinese term *ch'ien*, in the pronunciation *kan*, originally meant dry. Once conceived, the term then took on a life of its own, feeding on and being fed by those regions of the human mind that are given to abstractions, and whose awakening we notice in just this conceptualizing process of the authors of the early layers of our Book. In the course of this development, the origin of the term has become more and more meaningless and eventually entirely forgotten. The Judgment text is then entirely derived from the concept; the image, in this case, does not play any part in it any more. And conversely, the concept has even intruded into the line texts. In our present version of the third line, the dragon has been interpreted out and the superior man has been substituted for him. And in the Image text the message is, as in other cases, in turn derived from this substitution.

The phenomenon that can be observed in the history of these texts can be likened to what Erich Neumann calls *die Schrumpfung des Himmels*. It is a shrinking of the image, or at least of its field of action. In it the progressive self-realization of the human mind is reflected. The image, once entirely dominant, is reduced to the role of a counterpart of the concept, linked or opposed to it as the case might be, and from the fertile interplay between the two, but not any more from the image alone, meaning is derived. As will be shown as we go along, in this polarity the role of the image is at times subservient, at times preponderant. In no case, however, has the language of the image become the forgotten language.

Another interesting example of a mythological reference is contained in Hexagram 36, *Ming-i*, Darkening of the Light, or, in de Bary's translation, Obscured Brightness.[20] The mythological reference here is not as obvious as in the first hexagram, but a closer look at the line texts makes it just about inescapable. We see here Obscured Brightness "during flight." This is a phrase that is used in exactly the same wording with regard to several specific birds in the Book of Songs. We see Obscured Brightness lowering its wings. In other words, Obscured Brightness, a concept no doubt, is behaving here like a bird. We see furthermore Obscured Brightness pecking at the Lord of Light's left thigh in the fashion of the bird of prey pecking at Prometheus when he was chained to the mountain. It is, as stated, almost inescapable to interpret this image as a mythological bird of prey that, in the sixth line, takes on an almost Luciferian character. What the name of this bird was is not stated—no myth or myth fragment survives in China telling us about such a bird. It has been proposed to see in the term *Ming-i*, Obscured Brightness, the name of the bird.[21] This is, I believe, a fallacy. There is no evidence whatsoever that there was ever any bird in China, natural or mythological, that went by this name. I would prefer to see in these texts again a superimposition of a concept on a mythological image. The concept as such is no doubt, as in the case of the first hexagram, derived from a specific moment within the mythological story, the wounding of the light or of the bringer of the light. The concept has then, again as in the first

20. Theodore de Bary in *Chinese Thought and Institutions*, ed. John K. Fairbank (Chicago: University of Chicago Press, 1957), p. 165.

21. Arthur Waley, "The Book of Changes," *Bulletin of the Museum of Far Eastern Antiquities* (Stockholm), 5 (1933):127; Nathan Sivin in *Harvard Journal of Asian Studies* 26 (1966):297–98.

hexagram, become entirely independent and has eventually entirely dislodged the name of the image. The image as such, however, remains and speaks its powerful language. I resist the temptation here to reconstruct the original myth. Suffice it to say that the specific aspects of this myth lead us into situations that are known from non-Chinese mythologies.

Much could be said about the interplay of image and concept in this particular instance. I only want to mention that on the surface it appears to be purely terminological. But in this way it became possible to link a mythological situation with a historical one; the situation of the house of Chou on the eve of the conquest. This is how Prince Chi got into the text, a Chou prince at the Shang court who only by playing the madman could escape the injury suffered by his relatives, including King Wen himself, the bringer of the light. Through this terminological interplay, the impact of the mythological image could be strengthened by reference to a historical situation that must have been in everybody's mind at the time when these texts were formulated.

There are other cases of still recognizable mythological imagery in the texts of the Book. The horse could be mentioned here, about which a little bit more will be said somewhat further on. And then there are a number of cases where mythological imagery can be suspected, but cannot be demonstrated any more. I only want to mention here the man from the shadows, *yu-jen*, the *homo teneber*, the dweller in the dark valley, a mythological landscape that occurs in the Book of Changes and the Book of Songs, and at several other places in early Chinese literature. Twice he appears to give unobtrusive support to people who need strengthening or consolation, once in the nine in the second place of Hexagram 10, *Lü*, Treading, where he teaches perseverance to a man treading a smooth and level course. And once in the nine in the second place of Hexagram 54, The Marrying Maiden, where a lonely and rejected girl again is taught perseverance so that finally she is able to see again, even

though only with one eve. The *homo teneber* is the topic of a piece
of rhyme prose by Lu Chi, a poet of the early fourth century A.D.:

There are in the world men from the shadows
Who stand angling at mysterious banks.
They dust their cloud crowns to leave the world,
They slip on their dark wrappers and stand motionless.
That is why, outside of reality, one cannot conceive their secret
And, pursuing the mundane, one will not be able to fret their waves.
The harshness of autumn cannot make their leaves fade,
And the fragrance of spring cannot make their flowers bloom.
Transcending the world of dust and the world of shades and
  free from the web of connections,
What has a mundane order to offer to them?[22]

To sum up: mythological imagery, or at least demonstrably
mythological imagery, is surprisingly scarce in the Book of
Changes. Another source for J imagery can however be mentioned
here, the folk poetry of that time. The line texts of Hexagram 53,
Chien, Gradual Progress, read:

6/1: The wild goose gradually draws near the shore.
     The little son has something to talk.
6/2: The wild goose gradually draws near the cliff,
     Eating and drinking in peace and concord.
9/3: The wild goose gradually draws near the plateau,
     The man goes forth and does not return,
     The woman carries a child but does not bring forth.
6/4: The wild goose gradually draws near the tree,
     Perhaps it will find a flat branch.
9/5: The wild goose gradually draws near the summit.
     For three years the woman has no child.
9/6: The wild goose gradually draws near the cloud heights,
     Its feathers can be used for the sacred dance.

In the original these lines read like parts of a perfect poem. They

22. *J-wen Lei-chü*, comp. Ou-yang Hsün (557–641 A.D.), *chüan* 36.

use the then customary poetic line of four words, and they rhyme perfectly. Now, two stanzas of the 29th song in the Book of Songs contain the identical image of the wild goose. The pertinent lines read in Waley's translation:

> The wild geese take wing; they make for the island.
> The prince has gone off and we cannot find him.
> He must be staying with you.
> [The "you" to whom this poem is addressed is a wayward girl.]
> The wild geese take wing, they make for the land.[23]
> The prince went off and does not come back.
> He must be spending the night with you.[24]

Not only do we have in these two passages the same images, they also use the same rhymes and in one pair of lines even identical words. There is no doubt that the Book of Songs and the Book of Changes drew here on the same source. What we encounter here in the J is thus an image that is also found in poetry. This image is a transformed nature image and has in our context taken on aspects one will not find in nature. A natural wild goose flies in flocks and not alone. And a gander will not forsake his mate. It is in both cases the uncommon gander, the gander who breaks away from the usages of his kind. It is however revealing what the Songs and what the Changes make of this image. Both stay close to the poetic image by stressing the forlorn mate, the Changes even more poignantly than the Songs. But then, the emphasis of the Songs is on the fickle male and his despicable girl friend, whereas the concept with which this image is confronted in the Changes is Gradual Progress, that is to say, the development and self-realization of the male even at the expense of the mate. Again, the concept grew out of the image, it is derived from the word *gradually*, characterizing the flight of the gander. But once developed, the concept imposes upon

23. This is the word translated as "plateau" in the version above.
24. Arthur Waley, *The Book of Songs* (London: G. Allen & Unwin, 1937), p. 38.

the image a meaning entirely different from the one in the poem.[25]

There are a number of other images common to the Changes and the Songs. There are, for instance, the oppressive creeping vines that occur in the six at the top of Hexagram 47, *K'un*, Oppression, and as an associative image in all three stanzas in the fourth Song. There is the calling crane of the nine in the second place of Hexagram 61, *Chung Fu*, Inner Truth, that occurs in two stanzas of the 184th Song, and there is the high flying little bird who meets disaster in Hexagram 62, six at the beginning and six at the top, which occurs in the third stanza of the 224th Song in just about the same words, in Waley's translation:

> There is a bird, flies high . . .
> Only to be cruelly slain.[26]

The word translated "cruel" by Waley is the word for "disaster, misfortune" of the *I*.

And then there are a number of lines in the Changes that, even though parallels in the Songs are not preserved, are most easily explained as passages taken from existing folk poetry. As an example I would like to refer to a line in the six in the fourth place of Hexagram 22, *Pi*, Grace. "A White horse comes, as if on wings."

This gets us back to the horse image, the usage of which is extremely complex in the Book of Changes. The horse, or rather the mare, occurs as an image in the Judgment text of Hexagram 2, *K'un*, The Receptive. The usage here goes back, no doubt, to a mythological situation of which later versions persist, in which the mare appears as the mate of the dragon.[27] What we meet here would

25. In his book *The Flight of the Wild Gander* (New York: Viking Press, 1969), Joseph Campbell traces the very same image in India, and demonstrates that it was used in a way closely related to that of the Changes. Compare also the "Gander Whose Seat Is in the Light," referred to by Mircea Eliade, *Shamanism* (New York: Pantheon Books, 1964), p. 405.

26. Waley, *Book of Songs*, p. 323.

27. See Rousselle, "Drache und Stute," pp. 6–17.

then be the oceanic horse that Jung discusses so beautifully in his *Symbols of Transformation*. This horse occurs in a number of situations in the Changes. It occurs in the six at the beginning of Hexagram 59, *Huan*, Dissolution, where help is brought with the strength of a horse in order to counteract the process of dissolution before it has even begun. It occurs in the six in the fourth place of the 61st hexagram, where the team horse has to be sacrificed for the sake of the integrity of the situation that calls for humility. It is probably the same horse that gets lost in the nine at the beginning of the thirty-eighth hexagram, Opposition, but returns on its own accord, and the good horse of six in the third place of Hexagram 26, *Ta Ch'u*, The Taming Power of the Great, which follows others even in a situation of danger. Doubt, however, whether all the horses in the Changes are of the same type is strengthened by the Judgment text of Hexagram 35, *Chin*, Progress, where a powerful prince is honored with horses in large numbers. It seems that another type of horse appears here, the steppe horse, whose image is expressed most powerfully in the book *Shuo-kua*, in whose systematized image tabulation horses of different characteristics are associated with the *Ch'ien* trigram and other male trigrams. I do not want here to go into the question of the affinity of these two types of horses, an affinity that might in part be original and in part mutually derived.

The white horse that comes as if on wings does so in a poetic passage that is presented in a somewhat deviant rhythmic pattern known also to the Book of Songs and again with perfect rhymes. The same pattern and the same rhyme also occur in several lines of Hexagram 3, *Chun*, Difficulty at the Beginning, where the six in the second place reads: "Difficulties pile up,/Horse and wagon part,/He is not a robber, he comes to woo."

The second verse is repeated in the six of the fourth place and the six at the top of the same hexagram, the last one ending in the line: "Bloody tears flow."

The twenty-second hexagram uses this pattern in the nine in the third place: "Graceful and moist." And in the sixth in the fourth place: "Grace or simplicity? A white horse comes as if on wings,/ He is not a robber, he comes to woo."

It seems justified to assume that the quoted lines from these two hexagrams go back to the same poetic source. As no parallel version exists, it is not possible to trace the development of the imagery. It is obvious that we are again in both cases confronted with the phenomenon of the superimposition of the concept "difficulty" and "grace" on the image. The derivation of these concepts is less obvious. Possibly it is the unhitching of horse and wagon that led to the concept of difficulty, and the winged white horse that led to the concept of grace. How the somewhat forced courtship referred to in both cases, and which also occurs at the top line of Hexagram 48, *Ching*, The Well, fits into the poetic image, will have to remain a riddle. Confronted with the concept, the meaning becomes obvious. It leads in the first constellation, Difficulty at the Beginning, to at least temporary refusal and bloody tears and in the other to graceful acceptance.

We meet here the phenomenon of the same image leading to two different solutions when counterposed by two different concepts. With all due caution we might assume that in this case the double potential of the image grows out of its dynamics. The reality of change to which the Book owes its name works most stringently and most evidently in the images used in the line texts. These images do not represent a state of affairs or a mode of being; generally they develop and move on or, at least, show different facets and aspects. In other words, they are very much life entities. Conversely, the concepts are somewhat more static or at least conservative. The power of these properties works strongly at pulling the image into a specific position, attracting as it were one or the other aspect of its dynamic potential.

The phenomenon of a multiple application of the same image

under different constellations can then again be observed when we now turn to another source of imagery in the Book of Changes. At an earlier Eranos meeting we had occasion to discuss a few cases in which a historical event or a historical moment is brought into the line texts of the Book and is used as an image there.[28] The forcefulness of history, of the historical event, and, most of all, of the historical moment is brought home to us by these applications in the Book. We have, however, also to remind ourselves that in the historical eras we are talking about, the borderline between legendary and historical recording was occasionally vague to the point of being nonexistent. It was at times the intent rather than the execution that distinguished the ballad from the historical record. History thus used might have already gone through the hands of the mythopoeist or the ballad singer, and images occuring in these records might to a certain extent be akin to mythological images and images gathered from folk poetry.

In order to illustrate the question posed by our meeting, let me recall one or two of the historical references in the Book. You will remember the story of King Hai, that early Shang king who nomadized with his herds of sheep and cattle throughout northern China and was responsible for some economic innovations of great import, most importantly the hitching of cattle to pull carts, thereby contributing to the mobility of his wandering group. On his travels he then crossed the territory of the Lord of I, with whom immediate friendly relationships ensued until King Hai trespassed on the rules of propriety prevailing there regarding the female members of the Lord of I's household, and was in consequence punished by the Lord of I. This story is referred to twice in the Book, in Hexagrams 34, *Ta Chuang*, The Power of the Great, and 56, *Lü*, The Wanderer, in both instances as an associative rather than an evocative image. The main image of the thirty-fourth hexagram is, not surprisingly, the goat. Its goatiness, that is to say its

28. See pp. 56–62.

stubborn and inconsiderate drive to exercise physical force, gets the animal into a number of entanglements difficult of resolution. These ill-controlled scouts of the nomadic herds thus give contour to, and at the same time highlight, the specific dangers of the Power of the Great, both in outward procedure and in the personal characteristics of the one who exercises it. In the nine in the fourth place, the ruler of the hexagram, the entanglements created by the goats disappear and King Hai's story is brought in for the first time. "Power," it says here, "depends upon the axle of a big cart," King Hai's communicational mainstay. In the six in the fifth place a reference to another phase of the King Hai story is found. Here the goats are disposed of altogether and, even though this lot is not King Hai's choice but a punishment meted out by the Lord of I, no remorse accompanies the riddance of this embarrassment.

The image of the fifty-sixth hexagram is the Wanderer. In the top line of the hexagram, when sustenance for the specific way of life and the mission of the wanderer is destroyed due to illicit involvement on his side, the story of King Hai is brought in again. Here the king loses not just his goats but his cattle, and thereby the main support of his power. The fate of the wanderer coming to its end, when the wanderer's levity turns into laments and tears, cannot be better illustrated than by this phase of King Hai's story.

In passing, it is interesting to note that the fifty-sixth hexagram does not make use of a specific concept. The image of the wanderer is so strong, so versatile, and so emotive that the intended positions and constellations of this hexagram can be demonstrated in terms of the image alone.

This is not the only hexagram in which this specific type of image-concept relationship, that is to say the absolute dominance of the image, can be observed. In the thirty-fourth hexagram, The Power of the Great, the concept again is the one that pulled the image, in this case also the associative image, into place.

Similarly we find the story of the Emperor I of Shang giving his daughter in marriage to the chieftain of the Chou tribe occurring twice, in the fifty-fourth hexagram, The Marrying Maiden, and in the eleventh, Peace. Here we do not have two different phases of the same historical narrative, but two different aspects of the same historical moment thus used. In the fifty-fourth, again an entirely image-dominated hexagram, the emphasis is on the fate of the girl of whom an amount of self-denial is requested that is almost superhuman. In the eleventh, a concept-dominated hexagram, the emphasis is on the peace-yielding aspect of this fact and the blessings and the great good fortune that emanate from it.

This phenomenon of the multiple use of the same image has in the earlier layers of the Book never led to a stereotyped imagery. On the contrary, once an image was established as valid by contemplation, its many facets and vitality could be demonstrated only by multiple use. Once this usage was accepted, however, the development toward stereotyped images was a natural consequence. This development must have taken place at a rather early period. We then find images used almost like tropes, more or less automatically assigned to certain concepts and constellations. Particularly the trigrams have then become the receptacles of this stereotyped and systematized imagery. From earlier, still somewhat random, beginnings has then developed a system of coordinated imagery as we find it today laid down in the book *Shuo-kua*. Here we find the Creative associated with heaven, with the prince, with the father, and a great number of other images; and to all the other trigrams a large number of similarly systematized images accrued. Among them the animal images and the great nature symbols have assumed a most penetrating force. We find here the concept working not opposed to but within and through the images and their system. Conceptual thinking has led by that time to an insight into the regularity of certain situations expressed by images to a degree that these functional images, in being stereotyped, come close to playing the part of concepts. It must be observed, though, that the stereotyped place of these images does not in all cases coincide with their usage in the earlier layers of the Book. Thus, the dragon has been shifted from the Creative to the Arousing, the horse from the Receptive to the Creative and other male hexagrams, and so on. That means that the systematizing and conceptualizing process has imposed upon these images, or more cautiously, has rigidified certain inherent aspects of these images that the older layers have not, or not yet conceived. It has to be conceded that in this process a more developed and a more patternized society has worked into these conceptualized images certain social values and social attitudes of which they originally were innocent. The weight of a developing cultural and social heritage in its phenomenal manifestations attempts to assume in this way a validity that in the state of pristine purity belongs only to the images.

A closer scrutiny of these systematized images does, however, suggest that not even this process and its results have been as mechanical as the foregoing might indicate. This is not only said with the cognizance that no amount of conceptualization and social signification could quite cover up the immediate validity of these images, which were originally arrived at by contemplation and not by judgment. They too are the product of, or representations stemming from, a contemplating attitude. About this attitude, the Judgment text of Hexagram 20, *Kuan*, Contemplation, says that it is full of inner truth and as if looking up toward the object of contemplation; this unprepossessed and reverent attitude has led to an encounter also with these images and to their representation that no amount of systematized speculation can obscure. It is also said, bearing in mind that many, actually the greater number, of these system images have remained entirely free from any conceptualized overlays. If, for instance, it is said that various kinds

[215]

of black-billed birds are associated with the trigram Keeping Still, that the tortoise, the crab, the snail, the mussel, and the hawkbill tortoise are associated with the Clinging; that gray-haired men and men with broad foreheads are associated with the Gentle, which is the eldest daughter; that well-neighing horses and others are associated with the Arousing, whereas deep red, good, lean, old, and wild horses are associated with the Creative, and so on, no amount of speculation can apply these associations in a socially useful and desirable way.

Established social usages and the socially and politically useful and desirable, even though apparent to a slight degree in the later layers of the Book, were certainly not the determinants in the older layers. This will become surprisingly clear if we look at another source of imagery in the older layers. This point has to be emphasized. The generally assumed validity of the statements of the Book also outside of the cultural context of early China, the claim of the Wings that the Book is not bound to a certain place and a certain time, can be sustained only if, after close scrutiny, this point can be borne out.

This does not mean that the authors of the earlier layers disregarded the so-called facts of life, including the social and political facts. On the contrary, they faced the world they were living in with an astonishingly pitiless realism. Social and political positions, institutions, and relationships when exposed to their contemplation were, however, stripped of whatever rigidity usage and codification had added to them; in other words, they too were seen as images. There is in itself nothing strange in the use of the social and political world, too, in the earlier layers of the Book as a source, even as one of the most important sources, of imagery. The patterns revealed in this world, to be sure, have gone through a developmental molding just as those revealed in history, in the world of art and mythology, but they too emerge from basic archetypal situations with specific attributes and aspects. And it is to these that contemplation applies. What is strange, however, is the degree of unencumbered freedom with which the world of the social and political is faced. We find, and I shall try to demonstrate this with a few examples, that attitudes and values connected through tradition or law with specific social and political manifestations are never considered binding in the Book, indeed, that they are not even found worthy to be talked about. Hierarchical thinking, which patterned these manifestations, has no validity in these texts. To clarify what I want to convey here: gain and loss are recognized as basic directions of flow in life, property as an institution worthy of protection is not. My favorite example in this respect is the situation where a wanderer filches a cow that a citizen had tethered to his fence. The only comment the Book has on this event is: The wanderer's gain is the citizen's loss.

The degree of freedom from institutionalized patterns of the older layers of the text might best be exemplified by the father image. The strong position of the father within the web of social relationships in traditional China does not have to be restated here. Much of this is already reflected in the Wings. In the systematized imagery of the trigrams, the father is correlated with *ch'ien* and, for that matter, with its most exalted aspect. In the words of the *Shuo-kua*: "The Creative is heaven, *therefore* it is called the father."[29] The most clear-cut exposition of this relationship is expressed in the T'uan Commentary to Hexagram 37, *Chia Jen*, The Family. It says here:

> The correct place of the woman is within; the correct place of the man is without. That man and woman have their proper places is the greatest concept in nature.
> Among the members of the family there are strict rulers; these are father and mother. When the father is in truth a father and the son

29. Wilhelm-Baynes, p. 274. Italics mine.

[217]

a son, when the elder brother is an elder brother and the younger brother a younger brother, the husband a husband and the wife a wife, then the house is on the right way.

When the house is set in order, the world is established in a firm course.[30]

This is straight utopian Confucianism, which is found in the same wording also at other places within the Confucian scriptures. The attitude the father can expect within this system is one of awe but, like heaven, also one of unquestioning trust. A touchingly warm reflection of this is found in one of the verses of the Great Treatise, which discusses the proper approach to the lines of the Book, and where it says at one point: "They also show care and sorrow and their causes. Though you have no teacher / Approach them as you would your father and your mother."[31]

In the older layers of the text the word *father* occurs only in one hexagram, in which an entirely different aspect of the father image comes to the fore. This is Hexagram 18, *Ku*, Work on What Has Been Spoiled. The term *ku*, whose graph shows a bowl in which worms are breeding, has been used in later times for a specific practice of black magic.[32] The prevalence of this practice in Chou times is not recorded; one might, however, assume that the uncanny graph already carried magical connotations at that time and would then in this hexagram refer to the magical influence of the deceased father, who appears here as the great spoiler. It is an unfortunate son who has to set right what the father has spoiled. He has to act with tact and firmness and no condoning is tolerated even in joyous situations unless he wants to invite humiliation for himself as well as for his father. No wonder that having gone through an ordeal of this kind the son does not want to serve kings

30. Cf. ibid., p. 570.
31. Cf. ibid., p. 349.
32. H. Y. Feng and J. K. Shryock, "The Black Magic Known in China as Ku," *Journal of American Oriental Society* 55 (1935):1–30.

and princes any longer whose affinities to the spoiling qualities of his father might just be too close for his liking, but sets himself higher goals. I resist the temptation to hold against this image of a father-son relationship that of the Greek and of Freudian myth.

The image of this hexagram is that uncanny process of decay indicated by its name. By associating the sorcerer-father with this decay, other aspects of the father image are implicitly invoked, including those inherent in the stereotyped, "conceptualized" father image maintained by the social institutions. These are nowhere referred to in the text of the hexagram; the specific difficulty of the son, however, his having to walk the razor's edge and avoid excessive vigor as well as excessive permissiveness, is due to his father's social position.

As mentioned, this is the only hexagram in which the word *father* is used. There are others in which the involvement of the father is tacitly comprised. This is, not surprisingly, the case in Hexagram 37, The Family. In this hexagram the maintenance of the texture of the family is entirely due to the mother. She bears the responsibility for the joys and the chores of family life, including the noise at the time when the boys get into their teens. At the climactic moment, then, enters papa "like a king," spreading awe but also "good fortune." Here, too, the father image is determined by the father concept.[33]

The clan may serve as another example of how images are drawn from social realities in the Book of Changes. The natural cohesiveness of the clan as a social group has since early Chou times contributed decisively to the stability of Chinese society. The clan as an institution rested, to begin with, of course, on the cleaving

---

33. When this was written, the study of Raymond de Becker, "L'archetype du père dans le livre Chinois des Mutation," *La Tour de Saint Jacques* (July-August 1956), pp. 37–53, had not yet been available to me. De Becker deals mainly with the first hexagram and related texts that, as he cautiously suggests, reflect the father archetype.

brought about by kin relationships. It was reinforced by religious sanctions. The Chinese word for clan, *tsung*, originally meant the ancestor not so much in the sense of the physical forbear (this would be *tsu*) as in the sense of a religiously revealed fountainhead of clan cohesion and clan tradition. The graph shows something revealed out of a cave and is connected with the oldest layers of Chinese religious beliefs, in which deities and deified ancestors dwelled in mountain caves. The political order instituted by the early Chou is to an overwhelming extent based on the clan idea, and clan cohesion is also stressed in the Analects of Confucius, among other places.[34] The word is used twice in the Book of Changes. The first time it appears in Hexagram 13, *T'ung Jen*, Fellowship with Men, where among different types of fellowship groups the clan is mentioned, and where fellowship with men in the clan is pronounced humiliating. This pronouncement does, of course, fly in the face of the then existing political and social rules and customs. But again we have to marvel at the unencumbered mind of the authors of these texts who were able to see through the thicket of judgments and conventions, and recognize the dangers and mortifications of clannishness.

Even acknowledging that this pronouncement refers to a very specific situation, it appears that clan cohesion as such is considered a forced, and not a natural relationship. There is this strange text of the six in the fifth place of Hexagram 38, Opposition: "That clan fellow bites his way through the wrappings. If one goes to him,/How could it be a mistake?"[35]

Thus, even in this extraordinary situation, when natural instinct indicates association with one who has overcome his difficulties, this has to be specifically excused.

From the foregoing, I hope, a certain amount of understanding,

34. *Lun-yü* 8.2. Arthur Waley, *The Analects of Confucius* (London: G. Allen & Unwin, 1938), p. 132.
35. Cf. Wilhelm-Baynes, p. 150.

although incomplete, can be achieved of the intimate interplay of concept and image, the great polarity within the human mind. It can, at the least, be said that this interplay works out differently in any given situation. No formula can be built to cover their functional relationship. It cannot even be said that the concept acts normatively and the image emotively. In their continuous interrelationship positions and roles are constantly changed. The intricate tensions within the human mind created by this polarity reflect, as they are reflected by, what the Great Treatise calls "the confused diversities under Heaven."

INDEX

Publications on Asia of the Institute
for Comparative and Foreign Area Studies

1. Boyd Compton, trans. and ed. *Mao's China: Party Reform Documents, 1942–44.* 1952. Reissued 1966. Washington Paperback–4, 1966. 330 pp., map.

2. Siang-tseh Chiang. *The Nien Rebellion.* 1954. 177 pp., bibliog., index, maps.

3. Chung-li Chang. *The Chinese Gentry: Studies on Their Role in Nineteenth-Century Chinese Society.* Introduction by Franz Michael. 1955. Reissued 1967. Washington Paperback on Russia and Asia–4. 277 pp., bibliog., index, tables.

4. *Guide to the Memorials of Seven Leading Officials of Nineteenth-Century China.* Summaries and indexes of memorials to Hu Lin-i, Tseng Kuo-fan, Tso Tsung-tang, Kuo Sung-tao, Tseng Kuo-ch'üan, Li Hung-chang, Chang Chih-tung. 1955. 457 pp., mimeographed. Out of print.

5. Marc Raeff. *Siberia and the Reforms of 1822.* 1956. 228 pp., maps, bibliog., index. Out of print.

6. Li Chi. *The Beginnings of Chinese Civilization: Three Lectures Illustrated with Finds at Anyang.* 1957. Reissued 1968. Washington Paperback on Russia and Asia–6. 141 pp., illus., bibliog., index.

7. Pedro Carrasco. *Land and Polity in Tibet.* 1959. 318 pp., maps, bibliog., index.

8. Kung-chuan Hsiao. *Rural China: Imperial Control in the Nineteenth Century.* 1960. Reissued 1967. Washington Paperback on Russia and Asia–3. 797 pp., tables, bibliog., index.

9. Tso-liang Hsiao. *Power Relations within the Chinese Communist Movement, 1930–34.* Vol. I: *A Study of Documents.* 1961. 416 pp., bibliog., index, glossary. Vol. II: *The Chinese Documents.* 1967. 856 pp.

10. Chung-li Chang. *The Income of the Chinese Gentry.* Introduction by Franz Michael. 1962. 387 pp., tables, bibliog., index.

11. John M. Maki. *Court and Constitution in Japan: Selected Supreme Court Decisions, 1948–60.* 1964. 491 pp., bibliog., index.

12. Nicholas Poppe, Leon Hurvitz, and Hidehiro Okada. *Catalogue of the Manchu-Mongol Section of the Toyo Bunko.* 1964. 391 pp., index.

13. Stanley Spector. *Li Hung-chang and the Huai Army: A Study in*

Nineteenth-Century Chinese Regionalism. Introduction by Franz Michael. 1964. 399 pp., maps, tables, bibliog., glossary, index.

14. Franz Michael and Chung-li Chang. *The Taiping Rebellion: History and Documents.* Vol. I: *History.* 1966. 256 pp., maps, index. Vols. II and III: *Documents and Comments.* 1971. 756, 1,107 pp.

15. Vincent Y. C. Shih. *The Taiping Ideology: Its Sources, Interpretations, and Influences.* 1967. 576 pp., bibliog., index.

16. Nicholas Poppe. *The Twelve Deeds of Buddha: A Mongolian Version of the Lalitavistara: Mongolian Text, Notes, and English Translation.* 1967. 241 pp., illus. Paper.

17. Tsi-an Hsia. *The Gate of Darkness: Studies on the Leftist Literary Movement in China.* Preface by Franz Michael. Introduction by C. T. Hsia. 1968. 298 pp., index.

18. Tso-liang Hsiao. *The Land Revolution in China, 1930–1934: A Study of Documents.* 1969. 374 pp., tables, glossary, bibliog., index.

19. Michael Gasster. *Chinese Intellectuals and the Revolution of 1911: The Birth of Modern Chinese Radicalism.* 1969. 320 pp., glossary, bibliog., index.

20. Richard C. Thornton. *The Comintern and the Chinese Communists, 1928–31.* 1969. 266 pp., bibliog., index.

21. Julia C. Lin. *Modern Chinese Poetry: An Introduction.* 1972. 278 pp., bibliog., index.

22. Philip C. Huang. *Liang Ch'i-ch'ao and Modern Chinese Liberalism.* 1972. 200 pp., illus., glossary, bibliog., index.

23. Edwin Gerow and Margery Lang, eds. *Studies in the Language and Culture of South Asia.* 1974. 174 pp.

24. Barrie M. Morrison. *Lalmai, A Cultural Center of Early Bengal.* 1974. 190 pp., maps, drawings, tables.

25. Kung-chuan Hsiao. *A Modern China and a New World: K'ang Yu-Wei, Reformer and Utopian, 1858–1927.* 1975. 669 pp., transliteration table, bibliog., index.

26. Marleigh Grayer Ryan. *The Development of Realism in the Fiction of Tsubouchi Shōyō.* 1975. 133 pp., index.

27. Dae-Sook Suh and Chae-Jin Lee, eds. *Political Leadership in Korea.* 1976. 272 pp., tables, figures, index.

28. Hellmut Wilhelm. *Heaven, Earth, and Man in the Book of Changes: Seven Eranos Lectures.* 1976.

29. Jing-shen Tao. *The Jurchen in Twelfth-Century China: A Study of*

Sinicization. 1976. 217 pp., map, illus., appendix, glossary, bibliog., index.

30. Byung-joon Ahn. *Chinese Politics and the Cultural Revolution: Dynamics of Policy Processes, 1958–1966*. 1976.

31. Margaret Nowak and Stephen Durrant. *The Tale of the Nišan Shamaness: A Manchu Folk Epic*. Forthcoming.

32. Jerry Norman. *A Manchu-English Lexicon*. Forthcoming.